Laboratory Manual

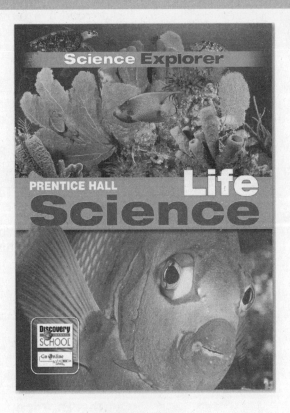

Science Explorer

PRENTICE HALL

Life Science

PEARSON

Prentice Hall

Boston, Massachusetts
Upper Saddle River, New Jersey

ISBN 0-13-190199-0   3 4 5 6 7 8 9 10 09 08 07 06

Safety Reviewers

W. H. Breazeale, Ph.D.
Department of Chemistry
College of Charleston
Charleston, South Carolina

Ruth Hathaway, Ph.D.
Hathaway Consulting
Cape Girardeau, Missouri

Douglas Mandt, M.S.
Science Education Consultant
Edgewood, Washington

Field Testers

Tom Barner
F. A. Day Middle School
Newton, Massachusetts

Nicki Bibbo
Witchcraft Heights School
Salem, Massachusetts

Rose-Marie Botting
Broward County School District
Fort Lauderdale, Florida

Colleen Campos
Laredo Middle School
Aurora, Colorado

Elizabeth Chait
W. L. Chenery Middle School
Belmont, Massachusetts

Holly Estes
Hale Middle School
Stow, Massachusetts

Laura Hapgood
Plymouth Community Intermediate School
Plymouth, Massachusetts

Mary F. Lavin
Plymouth Community Intermediate School
Plymouth, Massachusetts

James MacNeil, Ph.D.
Cambridge, Massachusetts

Lauren Magruder
St. Michael's Country Day School
Newport, Rhode Island

Jeanne Maurand
Austin Preparatory School
Reading, Massachusetts

Tom Messer
Cape Cod Academy
Osterville, Massachusetts

Joanne Jackson-Pelletier
Winman Junior High School
Warwick, Rhode Island

Warren Phillips
Plymouth Public Schools
Plymouth, Massachusetts

Carol Pirtle
Hale Middle School
Stow, Massachusetts

Kathleen M. Poe
Fletcher Middle School
Jacksonville, Florida

Cynthia B. Pope
Norfolk Public Schools
Norfolk, Virginia

Pasquale Puleo
F. A. Day Middle School
Newton, Massachusetts

Anne Scammell
Geneva Middle School
Geneva, New York

Karen Riley Sievers
Callanan Middle School
Des Moines, Iowa

David M. Smith
Eyer Middle School
Allentown, Pennsylvania

Gene Vitale
Parkland School
McHenry, Illinois

Contents

Contents *(continued)*

Science Explorer · *Science Safety Rules*

Science Safety Rules

To prepare yourself to work safely in the laboratory, read the following safety rules. Then read them a second time. Make sure you understand and follow each rule. Ask your teacher to explain any rules you do not understand.

Dress Code

1. To protect yourself from injuring your eyes, wear safety goggles whenever you work with chemicals, flames, glassware, or any substance that might get into your eyes. If you wear contact lenses, notify your teacher.

2. Wear an apron or a lab coat whenever you work with corrosive chemicals or substances that can stain.

3. Tie back long hair to keep it away from any chemicals, flames, or equipment.

4. Remove or tie back any article of clothing or jewelry that can hang down and touch chemicals, flames, or equipment. Roll up or secure long sleeves.

5. Never wear open shoes or sandals.

General Precautions

6. Read all directions for an experiment several times before beginning the activity. Carefully follow all written and oral instructions. If you are in doubt about any part of the experiment, ask your teacher for assistance.

7. Never perform activities that are not assigned or authorized by your teacher. Obtain permission before "experimenting" on your own. Never handle any equipment unless you have specific permission.

8. Never perform lab activities without direct supervision.

9. Never eat or drink in the laboratory.

10. Keep work areas clean and tidy at all times. Bring only notebooks and lab manuals or written lab procedures to the work area. All other items, such as purses and backpacks, should be left in a designated area.

11. Do not engage in horseplay.

First Aid

12. Always report all accidents or injuries to your teacher, no matter how minor. Notify your teacher immediately about any fires.

13. Learn what to do in case of specific accidents, such as getting acid in your eyes or on your skin. (Rinse acids from your body with plenty of water.)

14. Be aware of the location of the first-aid kit, but do not use it unless instructed by your teacher. In case of injury, your teacher should administer first aid. Your teacher may also send you to the school nurse or call a physician.

15. Know the location of the emergency equipment such as the fire extinguisher and fire blanket.

16. Know the location of the nearest telephone and whom to contact in an emergency.

Heating and Fire Safety

17. Never use a heat source, such as a candle, burner, or hot plate, without wearing safety goggles.

18. Never heat anything unless instructed to do so. A chemical that is harmless when cool may be dangerous when heated.

19. Keep all combustible materials away from flames. Never use a flame or spark near a combustible chemical.

20. Never reach across a flame.

21. Before using a laboratory burner, make sure you know proper procedures for lighting and adjusting the burner, as demonstrated by your teacher. Do not touch the burner. It may be hot. Never leave a lighted burner unattended. Turn off the burner when it is not in use.

22. Chemicals can splash or boil out of a heated test tube. When heating a substance in a test tube, make sure that the mouth of the tube is not pointed at you or anyone else.

23. Never heat a liquid in a closed container. The expanding gases produced may shatter the container.

24. Before picking up a container that has been heated, first hold the back of your hand near it. If you can feel heat on the back of your hand, the container is too hot to handle. Use an oven mitt to pick up a container that has been heated.

Science Explorer ▪ *Science Safety Rules*

Using Chemicals Safely

25. Never mix chemicals "for the fun of it." You might produce a dangerous, possibly explosive substance.

26. Never put your face near the mouth of a container that holds chemicals. Many chemicals are poisonous. Never touch, taste, or smell a chemical unless you are instructed by your teacher to do so.

27. Use only those chemicals needed in the activity. Read and double-check labels on supply bottles before removing any chemicals. Take only as much as you need. Keep all containers closed when chemicals are not being used.

28. Dispose of all chemicals as instructed by your teacher. To avoid contamination, never return chemicals to their original containers. Never pour untreated chemicals or other substances into the sink or trash containers.

29. Be extra careful when working with acids or bases. Pour all chemicals over the sink or a container, not over your work surface.

30. If you are instructed to test for odors, use a wafting motion to direct the odors to your nose. Do not inhale the fumes directly from the container.

31. When mixing an acid and water, always pour the water into the container first and then add the acid to the water. Never pour water into an acid.

32. Take extreme care not to spill any material in the laboratory. Wash chemical spills and splashes immediately with plenty of water. Immediately begin rinsing with water any acids that get on your skin or clothing, and notify your teacher of any acid spill at the same time.

Using Glassware Safely

33. Never force glass tubing or a thermometer into a rubber stopper or rubber tubing. Have your teacher insert the glass tubing or thermometer if required for an activity.

34. If you are using a laboratory burner, use a wire screen to protect glassware from any flame. Never heat glassware that is not thoroughly dry on the outside.

35. Keep in mind that hot glassware looks cool. Never pick up glassware without first checking to see if it is hot. Use an oven mitt. See rule 24.

36. Never use broken or chipped glassware. If glassware breaks, notify your teacher and dispose of the glassware in the proper broken-glassware container.

37. Never eat or drink from glassware.

38. Thoroughly clean glassware before putting it away.

Using Sharp Instruments

39. Handle scalpels or other sharp instruments with extreme care. Never cut material toward you; cut away from you.

40. Immediately notify your teacher if you cut your skin when working in the laboratory.

Animal and Plant Safety

41. Never perform experiments that cause pain, discomfort, or harm to animals. This rule applies at home as well as in the classroom.

42. Animals should be handled only if absolutely necessary. Your teacher will instruct you how to handle each animal species brought into the classroom.

43. If you know that you are allergic to certain plants, molds, or animals, tell your teacher before doing an activity in which these are used.

44. During field work, protect your skin by wearing long pants, long sleeves, socks, and closed shoes. Know how to recognize the poisonous plants and fungi in your area, as well as plants with thorns, and avoid contact with them. Never eat any part of a plant or fungus.

45. Wash your hands thoroughly after handling animals or a cage containing animals. Wash your hands when you are finished with any activity involving animal parts, plants, or soil.

End-of-Experiment Rules

46. After an experiment has been completed, turn off all burners or hot plates. If you used a gas burner, check that the gas-line valve to the burner is off. Unplug hot plates.

47. Turn off and unplug any other electrical equipment that you used.

48. Clean up your work area and return all equipment to its proper place.

49. Dispose of waste materials as instructed by your teacher.

50. Wash your hands after every experiment.

Science Explorer · *Science Safety Symbols*

Safety Symbols

These symbols appear in laboratory activities. They warn of possible dangers in the laboratory and remind you to work carefully.

Safety Goggles Wear safety goggles to protect your eyes in any activity involving chemicals, flames or heating, or glassware.

Lab Apron Wear a laboratory apron to protect your skin and clothing from damage.

Breakage Handle breakable materials, such as glassware, with care. Do not touch broken glassware.

Heat-Resistant Gloves Use an oven mitt or other hand protection when handling hot materials such as hot plates or hot glassware.

Plastic Gloves Wear disposable plastic gloves when working with harmful chemicals and organisms. Keep your hands away from your face, and dispose of the gloves according to your teacher's instructions.

Heating Use a clamp or tongs to pick up hot glassware. Do not touch hot objects with your bare hands.

Flames Before you work with flames, tie back loose hair and clothing. Follow instructions from your teacher about lighting and extinguishing flames.

No Flames When using flammable materials, make sure there are no flames, sparks, or other exposed heat sources present.

Corrosive Chemical Avoid getting acid or other corrosive chemicals on your skin or clothing or in your eyes. Do not inhale the vapors. Wash your hands after the activity.

Poison Do not let any poisonous chemical come into contact with your skin, and do not inhale its vapors. Wash your hands when you are finished with the activity.

Fumes Work in a ventilated area when harmful vapors may be involved. Avoid inhaling vapors directly. Only test an odor when directed to do so by your teacher, and use a wafting motion to direct the vapor toward your nose.

Sharp Object Scissors, scalpels, knives, needles, pins, and tacks can cut your skin. Always direct a sharp edge or point away from yourself and others.

Animal Safety Treat live or preserved animals or animal parts with care to avoid harming the animals or yourself. Wash your hands when you are finished with the activity.

Plant Safety Handle plants only as directed by your teacher. If you are allergic to certain plants, tell your teacher; do not do an activity involving those plants. Avoid touching harmful plants such as poison ivy. Wash your hands when you are finished with the activity.

Electric Shock To avoid electric shock, never use electrical equipment around water, or when the equipment is wet or your hands are wet. Be sure cords are untangled and cannot trip anyone. Unplug equipment not in use.

Physical Safety When an experiment involves physical activity, avoid injuring yourself or others. Alert your teacher if there is any reason you should not participate.

Disposal Dispose of chemicals and other laboratory materials safely. Follow the instructions from your teacher.

Hand Washing Wash your hands thoroughly when finished with the activity. Use antibacterial soap and warm water. Rinse well.

General Safety Awareness When this symbol appears, follow the instructions provided. When you are asked to develop your own procedure in a lab, have your teacher approve your plan before you go further.

Science Explorer • *Laboratory Safety*

Laboratory Safety Contract

I, _____ ,

(please print full name)

have read the Science Safety Rules and Safety Symbols sections, understand their contents completely, and agree to demonstrate compliance with all safety rules and guidelines that have been established in each of the following categories:

(please check)

❑ Dress Code

❑ General Precautions

❑ First Aid

❑ Heating and Fire Safety

❑ Using Chemicals Safely

❑ Using Glassware Safely

❑ Using Sharp Instruments

❑ Animal and Plant Safety

❑ End-of-Experiment Rules

_____

(signature)

Date _____

Science Explorer ▪ *Student Safety Test*

Student Safety Test: Recognizing Laboratory Safety

Pre-Lab Discussion

An important part of your study of science will be working in a laboratory. In the laboratory, you and your classmates will learn about the natural world by conducting experiments. Working directly with household objects, laboratory equipment, and even living things will help you to better understand the concepts you read about in your textbook or in class.

Most of the laboratory work you will do is quite safe. However, some laboratory equipment, chemicals, and specimens can be dangerous if handled improperly. Laboratory accidents do not just happen. They are caused by carelessness, improper handling of equipment, or inappropriate behavior.

In this investigation, you will learn how to prevent accidents and thus work safely in a laboratory. You will review some safety guidelines and become acquainted with the location and proper use of safety equipment in your classroom laboratory.

Problem

What are the proper practices for working safely in a science laboratory?

Materials *(per group)*

science textbook
laboratory safety equipment (for demonstration)

Procedure

Part A. Reviewing Laboratory Safety Rules and Symbols

1. Carefully read the list of laboratory safety rules listed on pages v and vi of this lab manual.

2. Special symbols are used throughout this lab book to call attention to investigations that require extra caution. Use page vii as a reference to describe what each symbol means in numbers 1 through 8 of Observations.

Part B. Location of Safety Equipment in Your Science Laboratory

1. The teacher will point out the location of the safety equipment in your classroom laboratory. Pay special attention to instructions for using such equipment as fire extinguishers, eyewash fountains, fire blankets, safety showers, and items in first-aid kits. Use the space provided in Part B under Observations to list the location of all safety equipment in your laboratory.

Science Explorer ▪ *Student Safety Test*

Recognizing Laboratory Safety *(continued)*

Observations

Part A

1. _____
   _____
   _____

2. _____
   _____
   _____

3. _____
   _____
   _____

4. _____
   _____
   _____

5. _____
   _____
   _____

6. _____
   _____
   _____

7. _____
   _____
   _____

8. _____
   _____
   _____

Science Explorer ▪ *Student Safety Test*

Part B

_____
_____
_____
_____
_____
_____

Analyze and Conclude

Look at each of the following drawings and explain why the laboratory activities pictured are unsafe.

1. _____
   _____
   _____
   _____

2. _____
   _____
   _____

3. _____
   _____
   _____
   _____

Science Explorer ▪ *Student Safety Test*

Recognizing Laboratory Safety *(continued)*

Critical Thinking and Applications

In each of the following situations, write *yes* if the proper safety procedures are being followed and *no* if they are not. Then give a reason for your answer.

1. Gina is thirsty. She rinses a beaker with water, refills it with water, and takes a drink.

_____

_____

_____

2. Bram notices that the electrical cord on his microscope is frayed near the plug. He takes the microscope to his teacher and asks for permission to use another one.

_____

_____

3. The printed directions in the lab book tell a student to pour a small amount of hydrochloric acid into a beaker. Jamal puts on safety goggles before pouring the acid into the beaker.

_____

_____

4. It is rather warm in the laboratory during a late spring day. Anna slips off her shoes and walks barefoot to the sink to clean her glassware.

_____

_____

5. While washing glassware, Mike splashes some water on Evon. To get even, Evon splashes him back.

_____

_____

6. During an experiment, Lindsey decides to mix two chemicals that the lab procedure does not say to mix, because she is curious about what will happen.

_____

_____

Name _____ Date _____ Class _____

Laboratory Skills Checkup 1

Following Directions

1. Read all of the following directions before you do anything.

2. Print your name, last name first, then your first name and middle initial (if you have one), at the top of this page.

3. Draw a line through the word "all" in direction 1.

4. Underline the word "directions" in direction 1.

5. In direction 2, circle the words "your first name."

6. In direction 3, place an "X" in front of the word "through."

7. Cross out the numbers of the even-numbered directions above.

8. In direction 7, cross out the word "above" and write the word "below" above it.

9. Write "Following directions is easy" under your name at the top of this page.

10. In direction 9, add the following sentence after the word "page": "That's what you think!"

11. Draw a square in the upper right corner of this page.

12. Draw a triangle in the lower left corner of this page.

13. Place a circle in the center of the square.

14. Place an "X" in the center of the triangle.

15. Now that you have read all the directions as instructed in direction 1, follow directions 2 and 16 only.

16. Please do not give away what this test is about by saying anything or doing anything to alert your classmates. If you have reached this direction, make believe you are still writing. See how many of your classmates really know how to follow directions.

Name _____ Date _____ Class _____

Laboratory Skills Checkup 2

Defining Elements of Scientific Inquiry

Laboratory activities and experiments involve the process of scientific inquiry. Listed in the left column are the names of parts of this method. The right column contains definitions. Next to each word in the left column, write the letter of the definition that best matches that word.

_____ 1. Hypothesis

A. Prediction about the outcome of an experiment

_____ 2. Manipulated Variable

B. What you measure or observe to obtain your results

_____ 3. Responding Variable

C. Measurements and other observations

_____ 4. Controlling Variables

D. Statement that sums up what you learn from an experiment

_____ 5. Observation

E. Factor that is changed in an experiment

_____ 6. Data

F. What the person performing the activity sees, hears, feels, smells, or tastes

_____ 7. Conclusion

G. Keeping all variables the same except the manipulated variable

Laboratory Skills Checkup 3

Analyzing Elements of Scientific Inquiry

Read the following statements and then answer the questions.

1. You and your friend are walking along a beach in Maine on January 15, at 8:00 AM.

2. You notice a thermometer on a nearby building that reads −1°C.

3. You also notice that there is snow on the roof of the building and icicles hanging from the roof.

4. You further notice a pool of sea water in the sand near the ocean.

5. Your friend looks at the icicles and the pool and says, "How come the water on the roof is frozen and the sea water is not?"

6. You answer, "I think that the salt in the sea water keeps it from freezing at −1°C."

7. You go on to say, "And I think under the same conditions, the same thing will happen tomorrow."

8. Your friend asks, "How can you be sure?" You answer, "I'm going to get some fresh water and some salt water and expose them to a temperature of −1°C and see what happens."

Questions

A. In which statement is a **prediction** made? _____

B. Which statement states a **problem**? _____

C. In which statement is an **experiment** described? _____

D. Which statement contains a **hypothesis**? _____

E. Which statements contain **data**? _____

F. Which statements describe **observations**? _____

Science Explorer ▪ *Laboratory Skills Checkup 4*

Laboratory Skills Checkup 4

Performing an Experiment

Read the following statements and then answer the questions.

1. A scientist wants to find out why sea water freezes at a lower temperature than fresh water.

2. The scientist goes to the library and reads a number of articles about the physical properties of solutions.

3. The scientist also reads about the composition of sea water.

4. The scientist travels to a nearby beach and observes the conditions there. The scientist notes the taste of the sea water and other factors such as waves, wind, air pressure, temperature, and humidity.

5. After considering all this information, the scientist sits at a desk and writes, "If sea water has salt in it, it will freeze at a lower temperature than fresh water."

6. The scientist goes back to the laboratory and does the following:
   a. Fills each of two beakers with 1 liter of fresh water.
   b. Dissolves 35 grams of table salt in one of the beakers.
   c. Places both beakers in a freezer at a temperature of −1°C.
   d. Leaves the beakers in the freezer for 24 hours.

7. After 24 hours, the scientist examines both beakers and finds the fresh water to be frozen. The salt water is still liquid.

8. The scientist writes in a notebook, "It appears that salt water freezes at a lower temperature than fresh water does."

9. The scientist continues, "I suggest that the reason sea water freezes at a lower temperature is that sea water contains dissolved salts, while fresh water does not."

Questions

A. Which statement(s) contain **conclusions**? _____

B. Which statement(s) contains a **hypothesis**? _____

C. Which statement(s) contain **observations**? _____

D. Which statement(s) describe an **experiment**? _____

E. In which statement is the **problem** described? _____

F. Which statement(s) contain **data**? _____

G. Which is the **manipulated variable** in the experiment? _____

H. What is the **responding variable** in the experiment? _____

Science Explorer ▪ *Laboratory Skills Checkup 5*

Laboratory Skills Checkup 5

Identifying Errors

Read the following paragraph and then answer the questions.

Andrew arrived at school and went directly to his earth science class. He took off his cap and coat and sat down at his desk. His teacher gave him a large rock and asked him to find its density. Realizing that the rock was too large to work with, Andrew got a hammer from the supply cabinet and hit the rock several times until he broke off a chip small enough to work with. He partly filled a graduated cylinder with water and suspended the rock in the water. The water level rose 2 cm. Andrew committed this measurement to memory. He next weighed the rock on a balance. The rock weighed 4 oz. Andrew then calculated the density of the rock as follows: He divided 2 cm by 4 oz. He then reported to his teacher that the density of the rock was .5 cm/oz.

Questions

1. What safety rule(s) did Andrew break? _____

_____

2. What mistake did Andrew make using measurement units?

_____

_____

3. What should Andrew have done with his data rather than commit them to memory?

_____

_____

4. What is wrong with the statement "He next weighed the rock on a balance"?

_____

_____

5. Why is "4 oz" an inappropriate measurement in a science experiment?

_____

_____

6. What mistake did Andrew make in calculating density?

_____

_____

Introduction to Life Science • *Design Your Own Lab*

Keeping Flowers Fresh

Problem

How can cut flowers stay fresher for a longer time?

Skills Focus

developing hypotheses, designing experiments, drawing conclusions

Materials

plastic cups

cut flowers

spoon

water

sugar

Procedure ✂ *Review the safety guidelines in Appendix A.*

1. You have just been given a bouquet of cut flowers. You remember once seeing a gardener put some sugar into the water in a vase before putting flowers in. You wonder if the gardener did that so that the flowers would stay fresh longer. Write a hypothesis for an experiment you could perform to answer your question.

    _____

    _____

2. Working with a partner, design a controlled experiment to test your hypothesis. Brainstorm a list of all the variables you will need to control. Also decide what data you will need to collect. For example, you could count the number of petals each flower drops. Then write out a detailed experimental plan for your teacher to review.

    Variables you need to control:

    _____

    _____

    _____

    _____

Introduction to Life Science ▪ *Design Your Own Lab*

Keeping Flowers Fresh *(continued)*

Manipulated variable:

_____

Responding variable:

_____

Data you will collect:

_____

_____

_____

_____

Experimental plan:

_____

_____

_____

_____

_____

_____

_____

3. If necessary, revise your plan according to your teacher's instructions. Then set up your experiment and begin collecting your data.

Analyze and Conclude

1. **Developing Hypotheses** What hypothesis did you decide to test? On what information or experience was your hypothesis based?

_____

_____

_____

2. **Designing Experiments** What was the manipulated variable in the experiment you performed? What was the responding variable? What variables were kept constant?

_____

_____

_____

Introduction to Life Science ▪ *Design Your Own Lab*

3. **Graphing** Use the data you collected to create one or more graphs of your experimental results. Create your graphs on separate pieces of graph paper. (For more on creating graphs, see the Skills Handbook in your textbook.) What patterns or trends do your graphs reveal?

_____

_____

_____

4. **Drawing Conclusions** Based on your graphs, what conclusion can you draw about sugar and cut flowers? Do your results support your hypothesis? Why or why not?

_____

_____

_____

_____

5. **Communicating** In a paragraph, describe which aspects of your experimental plan were difficult to carry out. Were any variables hard to control? Was it difficult to collect accurate data? What changes could you make to improve your experimental plan?

_____

_____

_____

_____

_____

More to Explore

Make a list of some additional questions you would like to investigate about how to keep cut flowers fresh. Choose one of the questions and write a hypothesis for an experiment you could perform. Then design a controlled experiment to test your hypothesis. *Obtain your teacher's permission before carrying our your investigation.*

Introduction to Life Science ▪ *Laboratory Investigation*

Using Scientific Inquiry to Investigate Potato Sprouting

Problem

How can you use the process of scientific inquiry to investigate whether light is necessary to the sprouting of a potato?

Skills Focus

observing, controlling variables, interpreting data, drawing conclusions

Materials

1 medium-sized potato, 2 plastic bags with twist ties, knife, 2 paper towels, marker pen

Procedure 🔲 ✂️ *Review the safety guidelines in Appendix A of your textbook.*

1. With members of your group, discuss whether a potato needs light to sprout. Based on your discussion, develop and record a hypothesis.

   _____

   _____

   _____

2. Use the marker pen to label one plastic bag as Potato A and the other plastic bag as Potato B. Also, use the marker pen to write the name of your group on each bag. Keep in mind that you will be making your observations through the bag; make sure your labels will not block your observations.

3. Fold each paper towel repeatedly until you have a rectangle about the same size as your potato halves. Moisten the towels with water. Place a folded towel in each plastic bag.

4. Carefully cut the potato in half lengthwise. Place a potato half in each plastic bag, with the cut surface of the potato on the paper towel.

5. Tie each bag with a twist. Each bag should look like the illustration on this page.

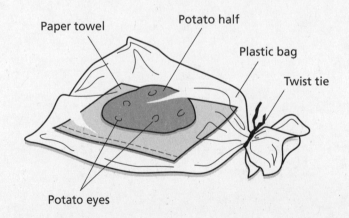

Paper towel · Potato half · Plastic bag · Twist tie · Potato eyes

Introduction to Life Science ▪ *Laboratory Investigation*

6. Count the number of eyes on each potato half. Record the number of eyes or sprouts, if any, in the Data Table.

Data Table

Potato	Number of Eyes	Number of Sprouts	
		Week 1	Week 2
Potato A			
Potato B			

7. Place Potato A in a place that receives light. Place Potato B in a dark place that receives little or no light. Be sure that the potato halves remain on top of the paper towels and that both potato halves are kept at the same temperature.

8. After 1 week, count the number of sprouts on each potato half. Record these data in the Data Table.

Analyze and Conclude

1. What was the manipulated variable and the responding variable in this experiment?

   _____

   _____

   _____

2. What variables were kept constant in this experiment?

   _____

   _____

   _____

3. Which potato had a greater percentage of sprouts—the potato kept in the dark or on the potato that received light?

   _____

   _____

4. Did your results support or disprove your hypothesis? Explain.

   _____

   _____

   _____

   _____

   _____

Introduction to Life Science ▪ *Laboratory Investigation*

Using Scientific Inquiry to Investigate Potato Sprouting *(continued)*

Critical Thinking and Applications

5. Why was it important to keep both Potato A and Potato B at the same temperature throughout the experiment?

_____

_____

_____

_____

_____

6. Why were the plastic bags sealed?

_____

_____

_____

7. Would your experimental results be enough to develop a scientific theory about potato sprouting? Explain.

_____

_____

_____

_____

_____

_____

More to Explore

Make a list of some additional questions you would like to investigate about what factors affect potato sprouting. Choose one of the questions and write a hypothesis for an experiment you could perform. Then design a controlled experiment to test your hypothesis. *Obtain your teacher's permission before carrying out your investigation.*

Living Things · *Skills Lab*

Please Pass the Bread!

Problem

What factors are necessary for bread molds to grow?

Skills Focus

observing, controlling variables

Materials

paper plates	sealable plastic bags
plastic dropper	tap water
bread without preservatives	packing tape

Procedure

1. Brainstorm with others to predict which factors might affect the growth of bread mold. Record your ideas.

2. Place two slices of bread of the same size and thickness on separate, clean plates.

3. To test the effect of moisture on bread mold growth, add drops of tap water to one bread slice until the whole slice is moist. Keep the other slice dry. Expose both slices to the air for one hour.

4. Put each slice into its own sealable bag. Press the outside of each bag to remove the air. Seal the bags. Then use packing tape to seal the bags again. Store the bags in a warm, dark place.

5. Record your observations in the data table.

6. Every day for at least five days, briefly remove the sealed bags from their storage place. Record whether any mold has grown. Estimate the area of the bread where mold is present. **CAUTION:** *Do not unseal the bags. At the end of the experiment, give the sealed bags to your teacher.*

Living Things · *Skills Lab*

Please Pass the Bread! *(continued)*

Data Table				
	Moistened Bread Slice		**Unmoistened Bread Slice**	
Day	**Mold Present?**	**Area with Mold**	**Mold Present?**	**Area with Mold**
1				
2				
3				
4				
5				

Analyze and Conclude

Write your answers on a separate sheet of paper.

1. **Observing** How did the appearance of the two slices of bread change over the course of the experiment?

2. **Inferring** How can you explain any differences in appearance between the two slices?

3. **Controlling Variables** What was the manipulated variable in this experiment? Why was it necessary to control all other variables except this one?

4. **Communicating** Suppose that you lived in Redi's time. A friend tells you that molds just suddenly appeared on bread. How would you explain to your friend about Redi's experiment and how it applies to molds and bread?

Design an Experiment

Choose another factor that may affect mold growth, such as temperature or the amount of light. Set up an experiment to test the factor you choose. Remember to keep all conditions the same except for the one you are testing. *Obtain your teacher's permission before carrying out your investigation.*

Living Things · *Technology Lab*

Design and Build a Microscope

Problem

How can you design and build a compound microscope?

Design Skills

building a prototype, evaluating design constraints

Materials

book

2 dual magnifying glasses, each with one high-power and one low-power lens

metric ruler

2 cardboard tubes from paper towels, or black construction paper

tape

Procedure

Part 1 Research and Investigate

1. Work with a partner. Using only your eyes, examine words in a book. Then use the high-power lens to examine the same words. In your notebook, contrast what you saw with and without the magnifying lens.

2. Hold the high-power lens about 5–6 cm above the words in the book. When you look at the words through the lens, they will look blurry.

3. Keep the high-power lens about 5–6 cm above the words. Hold the low-power lens above the high-power lens.

4. Move the low-power lens up and down until the image is in focus and upside down. (*Hint:* You may have to move the high-power lens up or down slightly, too.)

5. Once the image is in focus, experiment with raising and lowering both lenses. Your goal is to produce the highest magnification while keeping the image in clear focus.

6. When the image is in focus at the position of highest magnification, have your lab partner measure and record the distance between the book and the high-power lens. Your lab partner should also measure and record the distance between the two lenses.

7. On a separate sheet of paper write a description of how the magnified words viewed through two lenses compares with the words seen without magnification.

PART 2 Design and Build

8. Based on what you learned in Part 1, work with a partner to design your own two-lens (compound) microscope. Your microscope should

   ■ consist of one high-power lens and one low-power lens, each attached to a tube of paper or rolled-up cardboard

Living Things • *Technology Lab*

Design and Build a Microscope *(continued)*

- allow one tube to fit snugly inside the other tube so the distance between the two lenses can be easily adjusted

- focus to produce a clear, enlarged, upside-down image of the object you observe

- be made from dual magnifying glasses, cardboard tubes, and tape

9. Sketch your design on a sheet of paper. Obtain your teacher's approval for your design. Then construct your microscope.

PART 3 Evaluate and Redesign

10. Test your microscope by examining printed words or a printed photograph. Then, examine other objects such as a leaf or your skin. Record your observations. Did your microscope meet the criteria listed in Step 8?

11. Examine microscopes made by other students. Based on your tests and your examination of other microscopes, list ways you could improve your microscope.

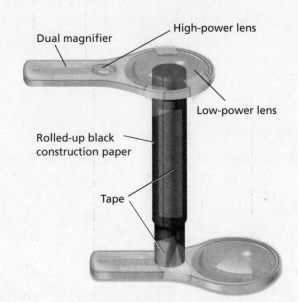

Dual magnifier

High-power lens

Low-power lens

Rolled-up black construction paper

Tape

Analyze and Conclude

Write your answers on a separate sheet of paper.

1. **Observing** Compare the images you observed using one lens with the image from two lenses.

2. **Evaluating Constraints** When you used two lenses, how did moving the top lens up and down affect the image? What was the effect of moving the bottom lens up and down?

3. **Building a Prototype** Describe how you built your microscope and explain why you built it that way.

4. **Evaluating the Impact on Society** Describe some of the ways that microscopes have aided scientists in their work.

Communicate

Imagine it is 1675. Write an explanation that will convince scientists to use your new microscope rather than the single-lens variety used by Leeuwenhoek.

Living Things · *Laboratory Investigation*

Developing a Classification System for Seeds

Pre-Lab Discussion

Suppose you discovered a plant or an animal that no one had ever seen. What would you call it? Where would you even begin?

To simplify the identification and naming of organisms, scientists have developed a system of classification. The classification system groups similar animals, plants, and other organisms. There are eight major levels of classification. The broadest group is a domain. Within a domain are kingdoms. Kingdoms contain phyla (singular *phylum*), classes, orders, families, genera (singular *genus*), and species. Organisms of the same species have the most characteristics in common.

In this investigation, you will develop a system of classification for seeds.

1. Why do scientists classify organisms into groups?

    _____

    _____

    _____

2. What can you infer if organism A shares three classification levels with organism B and five levels with organism C?

    _____

    _____

Problem

What characteristics can be used to classify seeds?

Materials *(per group)*

paper cup containing seeds   tray

2 hand lenses   metric ruler

scrap paper

Safety

Review the safety guidelines in Appendix A of your textbook.

Keep seeds in containers at all times to prevent accidents. Do not eat the seeds.

Procedure

1. Get a cup containing seeds. Carefully pour the seeds onto the tray. **CAUTION:** *Immediately pick up any seeds that drop on the floor.* Use a hand lens to examine the seeds carefully. Answer question 1 in Observations.
2. Think about what characteristic you could use to divide all the seeds into two large groups. Remember, each group must contain seeds with similar characteristics.
3. Sort the seeds into two piles, based on the characteristic that you selected. On scrap paper, note the characteristics that you choose.
4. Working with one of the two large groups, divide the seeds in that group into two smaller groups based on another characteristic. Record the characteristic as in Step 3.

Living Things • *Laboratory Investigation*

Developing a Classification System for Seeds *(continued)*

5. Continue to divide the seeds into smaller groups by choosing and recording new characteristics. Eventually, you should have only one seed left in each group.

6. Repeat steps 4 and 5 with the other large group.

7. In Observations, draw a diagram that shows how your classification system works.

8. Compare your classification system with those of other groups in your class. Answer questions 2–4 in Observations.

Observations

Diagram of Seed Classification

1. What are some of the characteristics of your seeds?

   _____

   _____

2. How many groups are in your classification system?

   _____

3. Compare the final classification system you have with those of other groups using different characteristics. Do they differ or are they the same? What different characteristics did they use?

   _____

   _____

   _____

Analyze and Conclude

1. What characteristics did you find most useful for classifying the seeds?

   _____

   _____

2. Explain why your final classification groups differed or were the same as those of other groups.

   _____

   _____

Living Things · *Laboratory Investigation*

3. How does a classification system help you understand organisms?

_____

_____

_____

4. How is this investigation similar to the way in which scientists classify organisms?

_____

_____

_____

Critical Thinking and Applications

1. Could you have classified your seeds using another system? Give a reason for your answer.

_____

_____

2. Could you have classified each characteristic in groups of three or more types at each step? Do you think more groups would make choices harder or easier? Give a reason for your answer.

_____

_____

_____

3. Suppose you wanted to classify all the birds that came to a particular area of a pond during a spring day. What are some of the characteristics that you would use to classify the birds?

_____

_____

4. When classifying organisms, do you think that it is better to go from general characteristics to specific characteristics or from specific characteristics to general characteristics? Give a reason for your answer.

_____

_____

_____

More to Explore

Make a list of five or more household appliances. Combine your list with a classmate's. Then separately devise classification systems for the combined list of appliances. What characteristics did you use to classify these items into groups? Did your classmate come up with the same classification system?

Name _____ Date _____ Class _____

Cell Processes and Energy ▪ *Consumer Lab*

Which Foods Are Fat-Free?

Problem

Some people wish to limit their intake of fats, or lipids. How can you determine whether information about fats on a food label is accurate?

Skills Focus

interpreting data, inferring

Materials

5 different snack dips in their containers, including nutrition labels

5 fat-testing strips with color key

permanent marker

5 cotton swabs

clock or watch

5 small squares of paper towel

Procedure

1. Record the brand names of the five snack dips in the data table. **CAUTION:** *Do not taste the dips at any time.*
2. Examine the nutrition label on the container of each dip. Record the percentage of the Daily Value (% DV) of fat that the dip contains.
3. Look at other information on the container to see whether the dip is labeled "fat-free." Record this information in the table.
4. Obtain five fat-testing strips. Label each strip with the name of one of the dips.
5. Use a cotton swab to smear a bit of one dip onto the test square of the corresponding testing strip. After 30 seconds, gently wipe the dip from the strip with a paper towel.
6. To determine whether the sample contains fat, compare the test square with the color key. Record your observation in the table.
7. Repeat Steps 5–6 for each of the sample dips.

Data Table			
Name of Dip	**Percent Fat (% Daily Value)**	**Labeled Fat-Free?**	**Result of Test**

Cell Processes and Energy ▪ *Consumer Lab*

Analyze and Conclude

1. **Observing** According to the information on the containers, which dips had 0% fat? Which dips were labeled "fat-free"?

   _____

   _____

   _____

2. **Interpreting Data** Did the result shown on the test square always agree with the information on the dip's container?

   _____

3. **Inferring** Based on your results, what can you conclude about the accuracy of labels indicating that foods are fat-free?

   _____

   _____

4. **Communicating** Write a report for consumers that summarizes your results. Summarize the processes you used.

   _____

   _____

   _____

   _____

   _____

Design an Experiment

Protein test strips indicate *how much* protein is present in a food sample. Design an experiment to rank five food samples in the order of least protein to most protein. *Obtain your teacher's permission before carrying out your investigation.*

Cell Processes and Energy ▪ *Skills Lab*

Multiplying by Dividing

Problem

How long do the stages of the cell cycle take?

Skills Focus

observing, calculating

Materials

microscope
colored pencils
calculator (optional)
prepared slides of onion root tip cells undergoing cell division

Procedure

1. Place the slide on the stage of a microscope. Use low power to locate a cell in interphase. Then switch to high power, and make a labeled drawing of the cell. **CAUTION:** *Slides and coverslips break easily. Do not allow the object to touch the slide. If the slide breaks, notify your teacher. Do not touch broken glass.*

2. Repeat Step 1 to find cells in prophase, metaphase, anaphase, and telophase.

3. Return to low power. Find an area of the slide with many cells undergoing cell division. Switch to the magnification that lets you see about 50 cells at once (for example, 100 ×).

4. Examine the cells row by row, and count the cells that are in interphase. Record that number in the data table on the next page under *First Sample.*

5. Examine the cells row by row four more times to count the cells in prophase, metaphase, anaphase, and telophase. Record the results.

6. Move to a new area on the slide. Repeat Steps 3–5 and record your counts in the column labeled *Second Sample.*

7. Fill in the column labeled *Total Number* by adding the numbers across each row in your data table.

8. Add the totals for the five stages to find the total number of cells counted.

Cell Processes and Energy ▪ *Skills Lab*

Data Table

Stage of Cell Cycle	First Sample	Second Sample	Total Number
Interphase			
Mitosis: Prophase			
Metaphase			
Anaphase			
Telophase			
Total number of cells counted			

Analyze and Conclude

1. **Observing** Which stage of the cell cycle did you observe most often?

   _____

2. **Calculating** The cell cycle for onion root tips takes about 720 minutes (12 hours). Use your data and the formula below to find the number of minutes each stage takes.

$$\text{Time for each stage} = \frac{\text{Number of cells at each stage}}{\text{Total number of cells counted}} \times 720 \text{ min}$$

3. **Communicating** Use the data to compare the amount of time spent in mitosis with the total time for the whole cell cycle. Write your answer in the form of a paragraph. Use a separate sheet of paper.

More to Explore

Examine prepared slides of animal cells undergoing cell division. Use drawings and descriptions to compare plant and animal mitosis.

Cell Processes and Energy ▪ *Laboratory Investigation*

Cell Membranes and Permeability

Pre-Lab Discussion

Can all substances move in both directions through a cell membrane? Why do some substances enter the cell through the cell membrane, while others do not? Sometimes you can use a model to answer questions like these. Part of this investigation models a living cell, so that you can observe changes that the cell membrane controls.

The cell membrane determines what diffuses into a cell. This characteristic of a cell membrane is called permeability. Many cells are semipermeable, which means that not all substances can pass through the cell membrane. Also, the amount of a substance that diffuses through a membrane is influenced by concentration and time.

In this investigation, you will model a cell membrane, determine if the membrane is permeable to certain substances, and find out if the concentration of a substance affects its diffusion.

1. Where is the cell membrane of a cell?

_____

_____

2. What types of materials pass through the cell membrane?

_____

_____

Problem

How does a cell membrane work?

Materials *(per group)*

plastic lunch bag
twist tie
100-mL graduated cylinder
starch solution
200-mL beaker
glass-marking pencil
water
iodine solution, three strengths
3 test tubes
test-tube rack
3 plastic cups
potato cubes
clock or watch with second hand
forceps
metric ruler

Cell Processes and Energy ▪ *Laboratory Investigation*

Safety 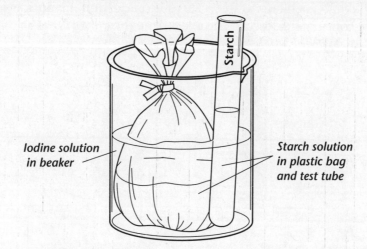 *Review the safety guidelines in Appendix A of your textbook.*

Iodine is poisonous. Keep it away from your face, and wash your hands thoroughly after using it. Iodine will stain your hands and clothing, so be careful not to spill it. Handle glass objects carefully. If they break, tell the teacher. Do not pick up broken glass.

Procedure

Part A: Model of a Cell Membrane

1. Write your name on a beaker with a glass-marking pencil. Then label three test tubes as follows: (1) "Iodine BEFORE," (2) "Iodine AFTER," and (3) "Starch."

Iodine solution in beaker

Starch solution in plastic bag and test tube

Figure 1

2. Fill the beaker with 40 mL of iodine solution. **CAUTION:** *Be careful with the iodine solution. If you spill any on yourself, immediately rinse the area with water and tell your teacher.* The iodine solution represents the environment outside the model cell.

3. Fill the test tube labeled "Iodine BEFORE" one-fourth full with iodine solution, and then set it aside in a test tube rack.

4. Fill a plastic lunch bag with 40 mL of starch solution, and seal the bag with a twist tie. Be careful not to spill starch onto the outside of the bag. Record the color of the solution in Data Table 1, and then place the bag into the solution in the beaker. The bag represents a cell.

5. Fill the "Starch" test tube about one-half full with starch solution, record the color of the solution, and then place the test tube in the beaker as shown in Figure 1. Let the beaker and its contents stand overnight.

6. The next day, remove the plastic bag and the test tube from the beaker. Record the colors of the solutions in the plastic bag and the test tube in the "Color AFTER" column in Data Table 1.

Cell Processes and Energy ▪ *Laboratory Investigation*

Cell Membranes and Permeability (continued)

7. Pour iodine solution from the beaker into the test tube labeled "Iodine AFTER" until the test tube has the same amount of solution as the test tube labeled "Iodine BEFORE."

8. Hold the two test tubes side by side, and look down through their openings. Record the colors of the solutions in the last line of Data Table 1.

Part B: Effect of Concentration on Diffusion

1. Label three plastic cups *100%*, *50%*, and *10%*.

2. Obtain about 30 mL of iodine solution at each strength, and pour that amount into the appropriate cup. Record these concentrations in Data Table 2.

3. Put a potato cube in each cup. If necessary, add additional solution to cover the cube completely. Record the exact time the cubes were added to the solutions in Data Table 2.

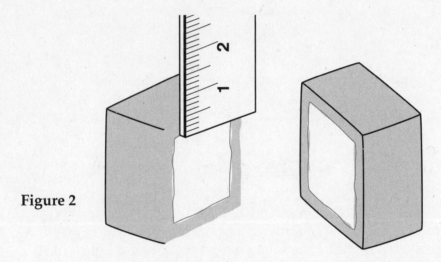

Figure 2

4. After 30 minutes, use forceps to remove each potato cube from its solution. Keep track of which sample was in which cup. The teacher will cut your potato cubes in half.

5. Use a metric ruler to determine the distance that the solution has diffused into each potato cube. See Figure 2. Read each distance to the closest 0.5 mm. In Data Table 2, record the distance that the solution diffused into each cube.

Cell Processes and Energy ▪ *Laboratory Investigation*

Observations

Data Table 1

Solution	Color Before	Color After
Starch in model cell		
Starch in test tube		
Iodine in test tubes		

Data Table 2

Potato Cube	Concentration of Substance	Distance of Diffusion (mm)
1		
2		
3		

Analyze and Conclude

1. What part of the cell does the plastic bag represent?

   _____

   _____

2. What was the purpose of placing a test tube containing starch solution in the beaker of iodine?

   _____

   _____

3. When starch mixes with iodine, the mixture turns blue. What can you infer about the contents of the plastic bag?

   _____

   _____

Cell Processes and Energy ▪ *Laboratory Investigation*

Cell Membranes and Permeability *(continued)*

4. **a.** Did starch move out of the bag? Give a reason for your answer.

   _____

   _____

   b. Did iodine move into the bag? Give a reason for your answer.

   _____

   _____

5. Based on your results, was the model cell membrane permeable or impermeable to iodine? To starch?

   _____

   _____

6. In Part B, how did the concentration of iodine influence the amount of diffusion that took place?

   _____

   _____

Critical Thinking and Applications

1. Cell membranes contain small holes, or pores. Pore size may determine why some chemicals can or cannot pass through a cell membrane. In your model, how might the size of the membrane pores compare to the size of the iodine molecules? Explain.

   _____

   _____

   _____

2. In your model, how might the size of the membrane pores compare to the size of the starch molecules? Explain.

   _____

   _____

   _____

3. Based on what you learned from studying the diffusion of different concentrations, what might be one reason that sick or injured people wear oxygen masks? Explain.

   _____

   _____

   _____

   _____

Cell Processes and Energy ▪ *Laboratory Investigation*

More to Explore

New Problem How does time affect the diffusion of substances across a cell membrane?

Possible Materials Consider which materials you can use from the previous part of the lab.

Safety Handle glass objects carefully. Ask your teacher to cut the potato cubes.

Procedure Develop a procedure to solve the problem. Predict what the results will show. Write your procedure on a separate sheet of paper. Have the teacher approve your procedure before you carry out the investigation.

Observations On a separate sheet of paper, make a data table in which to record your data and observations.

Analyze and Conclude Did your results support your prediction? Explain your reasoning.

_____

_____

_____

_____

Genetics: The Science of Heredity ▪ *Skills Lab*

Take a Class Survey

Problem

Are traits controlled by dominant alleles more common than traits controlled by recessive alleles?

Skill Focus

developing hypotheses, interpreting data

Materials

mirror (optional)

Procedure

PART 1 Dominant and Recessive Alleles

1. Write a hypothesis reflecting your ideas about the problem question.

   _____

   _____

2. For each of the traits listed in the data table on the next page, work with a partner to determine which trait you have. Circle that trait in your data table.

3. Count the number of students in your class who have each trait. Record that number in your data table. Also record the total number of students.

PART 2 Are Your Traits Unique?

4. Look at the circle of traits in your text. All the traits in your data table appear in the circle. Place the eraser end of your pencil on the trait in the small central circle that applies to you—either free ear lobes or attached ear lobes.

5. Look at the two traits touching the space your eraser is on. Move your eraser onto the next description that applies to you. Continue using your eraser to trace your traits until you reach a number on the outside rim of the circle. Share that number with your classmates.

Name _____ Date _____ Class _____

Genetics: The Science of Heredity · *Skills Lab*

Data Table				
Total Number or Students _____				
	Trait 1	Number	Trait 2	Number
A	Free ear lobes		Attached ear lobes	
B	Hair on fingers		No hair on fingers	
C	Widow's peak		No widow's peak	
D	Curly hair		Straight hair	
E	Cleft chin		Smooth chin	
F	Smile dimples		No smile dimples	

Analyze and Conclude

Write your answers in the spaces provided.

1. **Observing** The traits listed under Trait 1 in the data table are controlled by dominant alleles. The traits listed under Trait 2 are controlled by recessive alleles. Which traits controlled by dominant alleles were shown by a majority of students? Which traits controlled by recessive alleles were shown by a majority of students?

   _____

   _____

2. **Interpreting Data** How many students ended up on the same number on the circle of traits? How many students were the only ones to have their number? What do the results suggest about each person's combination of traits?

   _____

   _____

   _____

3. **Developing Hypotheses** Do your data support the hypothesis you proposed in Step 1? Write an answer with examples.

   _____

   _____

   _____

Genetics: The Science of Heredity ▪ *Skills Lab*

Take a Class Survey *(continued)*

Design an Experiment

Do people who are related to each other show more genetic similarity than unrelated people? Write a hypothesis. Then design an experiment to test your hypothesis. *Obtain your teacher's permission before carrying out your investigation.*

_____

_____

_____

_____

Genetics: The Science of Heredity ▪ *Skills Lab*

Make the Right Call!

Problem

How can you predict the possible results of genetic crosses?

Skills Focus

making models, interpreting data

Materials

2 small paper bags   marking pen
3 blue marbles   3 white marbles

Procedure

1. Label one bag "Bag 1, Female Parent." Label the other bag "Bag 2, Male Parent." Then read over Part 1, Part 2, and Part 3 of this lab. Write a prediction on another sheet of paper about the kinds of offspring you expect from each cross.

PART 1 Crossing Two Homozygous Parents

2. Place two blue marbles in Bag 1. This pair of marbles represents the female parent's alleles. Use the letter *B* to represent the dominant allele for blue color.

3. Place two white marbles in Bag 2. Use the letter *b* to represent the recessive allele for white color.

4. For Trial 1, remove one marble from Bag 1 without looking in the bag. Record the result in your data table. Return the marble to the bag. Again, without looking in the bag, remove one marble from Bag 2. Record the result in your data table. Return the marble to the bag.

5. In the column labeled Offspring's Alleles, write *BB* if you removed two blue marbles, *bb* if you removed two white marbles, or *Bb* if you removed one blue marble and one white marble.

6. Repeat Steps 4 and 5 nine more times.

PART 2 Crossing Homozygous and Heterozygous Parents

7. Place two blue marbles in Bag 1. Place one white marble and one blue marble in Bag 2.

8. Repeat Steps 4 and 5 ten times, and record your data in the data table for Part 2.

PART 3 Crossing Two Heterozygous Parents

9. Place one blue marble and one white marble in Bag 1. Place one blue marble and one white marble in Bag 2.

10. Repeat Steps 4 and 5 ten times, and record your data in the data table for Part 3.

Genetics: The Science of Heredity ▪ *Skills Lab*

Data Table: Part 1

Trial	Allele From Bag 1 (Female Parent)	Allele From Bag 2 (Male Parent)	Offspring's Alleles
1			
2			
3			
4			
5			
6			
7			
8			
9			
10			

Data Table: Part 2

Trial	Allele From Bag 1 (Female Parent)	Allele From Bag 2 (Male Parent)	Offspring's Alleles
1			
2			
3			
4			
5			
6			
7			
8			
9			
10			

Data Table: Part 3

Trial	Allele From Bag 1 (Female Parent)	Allele From Bag 2 (Male Parent)	Offspring's Alleles
1			
2			
3			
4			
5			
6			
7			
8			
9			
10			

Genetics: The Science of Heredity · *Skills Lab*

Make the Right Call! *(continued)*

Analyze and Conclude

Write your answers on a separate sheet of paper.

1. **Making Models** Make a Punnett square for each of the crosses you modeled in Part 1, Part 2, and Part 3.

2. **Interpreting Data** According to your results in Part 1, how many different kinds of offspring are possible when the homozygous parents (*BB* and *bb*) are crossed? Do the results you obtained using the marble model agree with the results shown by a Punnett square?

3. **Predicting** According to your results in Part 2, what percentage of offspring are likely to be homozygous when a homozygous parent (*BB*) and a heterozygous parent (*Bb*) are crossed? What percentage of offspring are likely to be heterozygous (*Bb*)? Does the model agree with the results shown by a Punnett square?

4. **Communicating** According to your results in Part 3, what different kinds of offspring are possible when two heterozygous parents (*Bb* × *Bb*) are crossed? What percentages of each type of offspring are likely to be produced? Does the model agree with the results of a Punnett square?

5. **Inferring** For Part 3, if you did 100 trials instead of 10 trials, would your results be closer to the results shown in a Punnett square? Explain.

6. **Communicating** In a paragraph, explain how the marble model compares with a Punnett square. How are the two methods alike? How are they different?

More to Explore

In peas, the allele for yellow seeds (*Y*) is dominant over the allele for green seeds (*y*). What possible crosses do you think could produce a heterozygous plant with yellow seeds (*Yy*)? Use the marble model and Punnett squares to test your predictions.

Genetics: The Science of Heredity ▪ *Laboratory Investigation*

Chromosomes and Inheritance

Pre-Lab Discussion

How are traits inherited? You can investigate this question by considering an imaginary animal called the unimonster. Suppose this animal has only one pair of chromosomes. Chromosomes carry genes, which control different genetic traits, such as hair color, height, and other physical characteristics. Different forms of a gene are called alleles. The presence of different alleles on the chromosomes of unimonsters determines whether they have one horn or two horns. During reproduction, parent unimonsters pass on alleles to their offspring.

In this investigation, you will determine the different allele combinations for the offspring of two unimonsters and figure out the number of horns the young unimonsters will have.

1. What are dominant and recessive alleles?

   _____

   _____

2. Define *genotype* and *phenotype*.

   _____

   _____

3. What does it mean to say that an organism is homozygous for a trait? Heterozygous for a trait?

   _____

   _____

4. How do the numbers of chromosomes in cells compare with the number of chromosomes in sex cells? During reproduction, what fraction of chromosomes does each parent contribute to its offspring?

   _____

   _____

Problem

How can you determine the traits of a unimonster's offspring?

Materials *(per group)*

marker
craft sticks

Genetics: The Science of Heredity ▪ *Laboratory Investigation*

Procedure

1. Figure 1 shows a mother and a father unimonster, each with different genetic traits. The allele for two horns is dominant over the allele for one horn. Look at the drawing and answer question 1 in Observations.

Mother Unimonster   Father Unimonster

Figure 1

2. The mother unimonster is heterozygous. This means that she has one allele for two horns and one allele for one horn. Each of her sex cells will have either a chromosome with the two-horn allele or a chromosome with the one-horn allele. Follow Figure 2 and steps 3 and 4 to make a model of the mother unimonster's sex chromosomes.

3. One of the mother unimonster's chromosomes will carry the two-horn allele. Write "M1" (for mother) at one end of a craft stick. At the other end of the stick, write *H* for the dominant two-horn allele.

4. The mother unimonster's other chromosome will carry the one-horn allele. Write "M2" at the end of a second stick. At the other end, write *h* for the recessive one-horn allele.

5. The father unimonster is homozygous *(hh)*. Follow Figure 2 to make models of the father's chromosomes: F1 and F2.

Figure 2

6. During reproduction, the sex cells produced by the mother and father unimonsters combine to form a fertilized egg. The fertilized egg will grow into a young unimonster. Whether the young unimonster has one or two horns depends on the alleles on the chromosome contributed by each parent during reproduction. In Observations, use your chromosome models to answer questions 2–5. Remember that the allele for two horns is dominant. Anytime the dominant allele *(H)* is present, the unimonster will have two horns.

Genetics: The Science of Heredity ▪ *Laboratory Investigation*

Chromosomes and Inheritance (continued)

Observations

1. Which unimonster parent has the dominant allele for number of horns? How do you know?

_____

_____

2. During reproduction, the sex cells containing the chromosomes M1 and F1 combine to form a fertilized egg.

   a. Which alleles are on each of the chromosomes?

   _____

   b. Will the young unimonster have one horn or two horns? Draw the appropriate number of horns on young unimonster 1 in Figure 3.

3. During reproduction, the sex cells containing the chromosomes M1 and F2 combine to form a fertilized egg.

   a. Which alleles are on each of the chromosomes?

   _____

   b. Will the young unimonster have one horn or two horns? Draw the appropriate number of horns on young unimonster 2 in Figure 3.

4. During reproduction, the sex cells containing the chromosomes M2 and F1 combine to form a fertilized egg.

   a. Which alleles are on each of the chromosomes?

   _____

   b. Will the young unimonster have one horn or two horns? Draw the appropriate number of horns on young unimonster 3 in Figure 3.

5. During reproduction, the sex cells containing the chromosomes M2 and F2 combine to form a fertilized egg.

   a. Which alleles are on each of the chromosomes?

   _____

   b. Will the young unimonster have one horn or two horns? Draw the appropriate number of horns on young unimonster 4 in Figure 3.

| Young Unimonster 1 | Young Unimonster 2 | Young Unimonster 3 | Young Unimonster 4 |

Figure 3

Genetics: The Science of Heredity • *Laboratory Investigation*

Analyze and Conclude

1. Which young unimonster(s) are homozygous and have one horn?

_____

_____

2. Which young unimonster(s) are heterozygous?

_____

_____

3. Are any young unimonster(s) homozygous with two horns? Explain.

_____

_____

Critical Thinking and Applications

1. If a mother unimonster is homozygous and has two horns, and a father unimonster is homozygous and has one horn, what are the phenotypes and genotypes of the possible offspring? Remember that the two-horn allele is dominant.

_____

_____

2. Predict the phenotypes and genotypes of the offspring of a mother unimonster and a father unimonster that are both heterozygous.

_____

_____

More to Explore

Repeat the lab for the traits of curly hair versus straight hair. Assume that the curly-hair allele is dominant and the straight-hair allele is recessive. The mother is homozygous and has straight hair, while the father is heterozygous. Get four more craft sticks. Make all the combinations of different alleles. Determine all of the possible genotypes and the resulting phenotypes of the offspring. You may wish to use the Punnett square below to record the genotypes.

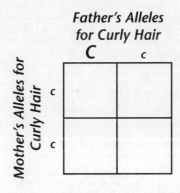

Modern Genetics ▪ *Skills Lab*

Family Puzzle

Problem

A husband and wife want to understand the probability that their children might inherit cystic fibrosis. How can you use the information in the labeled Case Study to predict the probability?

Skills Focus

interpreting data, predicting

Materials

12 index cards

scissors

marker

Procedure

1. Read the Case Study. In your notebook, draw a pedigree that shows all the family members. Use circles to represent the females, and squares to represent the males. Shade in the circles or squares representing the individuals who have cystic fibrosis.

2. You know that cystic fibrosis is controlled by a recessive allele. To help you figure out Joshua and Bella's family pattern, create a set of cards to represent the alleles. Cut each of six index cards into four smaller cards. On 12 of the small cards, write *N* to represent the dominant normal allele. On the other 12 small cards, write *n* for the recessive allele.

> ### Case Study:
> ### Joshua and Bella
>
> • Joshua and Bella have a son named Ian. Ian has been diagnosed with cystic fibrosis.
> • Joshua and Bella are both healthy.
> • Bella's parents are both healthy.
> • Joshua's parents are both healthy.
> • Joshua's sister, Sara, has cystic fibrosis.

3. Begin by using the cards to represent Ian's alleles. Since he has cystic fibrosis, what alleles must he have? Write in this genotype next to the pedigree symbol for Ian.

4. Joshua's sister, Sara, also has cystic fibrosis. What alleles does she have? Write in this genotype next to the pedigree symbol that represents Sara.

Modern Genetics · *Skills Lab*

5. Now use the cards to figure out what genotypes Joshua and Bella must have. Write their genotypes next to their symbols in the pedigree.

6. Work with the cards to figure out the genotypes of all other family members. Fill in each person's genotype next to his or her symbol in the pedigree. If more than one genotype is possible, write in both genotypes.

Analyze and Conclude

Write your answers in the spaces provided.

1. **Interpreting Data** What were the genotypes of Joshua's parents? What were the genotypes of Bella's parents?

   _____

   _____

2. **Predicting** Joshua also has a brother. What is the probability that he has cystic fibrosis? Explain.

   _____

   _____

   _____

3. **Communicating** Imagine that you are a genetic counselor. A couple asks why you need information about many generations of their families to draw conclusions about a hereditary condition. Write an explanation you can give to them.

   _____

   _____

   _____

   _____

More to Explore

Review the pedigree that you just studied. What data suggest that the traits are not sex-linked? Explain.

_____

_____

_____

_____

Modern Genetics · *Skills Lab*

Guilty or Innocent?

Problem

A crime scene may contain hair, skin, or blood from a criminal. These materials all contain DNA that can be used to make a DNA fingerprint. A DNA fingerprint, which consists of a series of bands, is something like a bar code. How can a DNA fingerprint identify individuals?

Skills Focus

drawing conclusions, inferring

Materials

4–6 bar codes
hand lens

Procedure

1. Look at the photograph of DNA band patterns shown in your text. Each person's DNA produces a unique pattern of these bands.

2. Now look at the Universal Product Code, also called a bar code, shown below the DNA bands. A bar code can be used as a model of a DNA band pattern. Compare the bar code with the DNA bands to see what they have in common. Record your observations on a separate sheet of paper.

3. Suppose that a burglary has taken place, and you're the detective leading the investigation. Your teacher will give you a bar code that represents DNA from blood found at the crime scene. You arrange to have DNA samples taken from several suspects. Write a sentence in the space below describing what you will look for as you try to match each suspect's DNA to the DNA sample from the crime scene.

_____

_____

4. You will now be given bar codes representing DNA samples taken from the suspects. Compare those bar codes with the bar code that represents DNA from the crime scene.

5. Use your comparisons to determine whether any of the suspects was present at the crime scene.

Modern Genetics · *Skills Lab*

Analyze and Conclude

Write your answers in the spaces provided.

1. **Drawing Conclusions** Based on your findings, were any of the suspects present at the crime scene? Support your conclusion with specific evidence.

   _____

   _____

   _____

   _____

   _____

2. **Inferring** Why do people's DNA patterns differ so greatly?

   _____

   _____

   _____

3. **Drawing Conclusions** How would your conclusions be affected if you learned that the suspect whose DNA matched the evidence had an identical twin?

   _____

   _____

   _____

   _____

4. **Communicating** Suppose you are a defense lawyer. DNA evidence indicates that the bloodstain at the scene of a crime belongs to your client. Do you think this DNA evidence should be enough to convict your client? Write a speech you might give to the jury in defense of your client.

   _____

   _____

   _____

   _____

   _____

More to Explore

Do you think the DNA fingerprints of a parent and a child would show any similarities? Explain your thinking.

Modern Genetics • *Laboratory Investigation*

How Are Genes on Sex Chromosomes Inherited?

Pre-Lab Discussion

Sex-linked genes are genes on the X and Y chromosomes. Traits controlled by these genes are called sex-linked traits. Two sex-linked traits include hemophilia and colorblindness. Hemophilia is a genetic disorder in which a person's blood clots slowly or not at all. If a person has the dominant allele X^H, he or she will have normal blood. If a person has only the recessive allele X^h, he or she will have hemophilia.

Red-green colorblindness is also a genetic disorder. In this disorder, the person does not see red and green properly. This person will see green as gray and red as yellow. If a person has at least one dominant allele X^C, he or she will not have colorblindness. If a person has only the recessive allele X^c, he or she will have colorblindness.

In this investigation, you will see how hemophilia and colorblindness are inherited.

1. How are the alleles for sex-linked genes passed from parent to child?

   _____

   _____

2. How many X and Y chromosomes do males have? How many of each do females have?

   _____

   _____

3. Define the carrier of a trait in terms of alleles.

   _____

   _____

Problem

How are hemophilia and red-green colorblindness inherited?

Materials *(per group)*

8 pennies
tape
pen
cloth to cover desktop

Modern Genetics · *Laboratory Investigation*

Procedure

Part A: Hemophilia

Use the following information and procedures for families
1 and 2 to model the inheritance of hemophilia. Keep in mind
that only the X chromosome can carry the allele for hemophilia.
A female can be $X^H X^H$, $X^H X^h$, or $X^h X^h$.
A male can be $X^H Y$ or $X^h Y$.

Figure 1

Coin 1
Male
Front   Back

Family 1. Parents do not have hemophilia; mother is a carrier
of hemophilia ($X^H X^h$)

1. Place tape on two coins and mark them as shown in
   Figure 1. These coins represent the alleles of the parents.
   The coin with the Y chromosome on the back is the father.
   The coin with an X on each side is the mother.

Coin 2
Female
Front   Back

2. Spread out a piece of cloth on your desk or tabletop. Shake
   the coins in your hands and drop them onto the cloth.

3. Read the combination of letters that appears. This
   combination represents the result that might appear in a
   child of these parents.

Figure 2

Coin 3
Male
Front   Back

4. Use a tally mark in the correct row to record this combination
   of alleles in Data Table 1 in the column marked "Children
   Observed."

Coin 4
Female
Front   Back

5. Repeat shaking, dropping, reading, and tallying the coins a
   total of 40 times. Record the totals of tally marks for each
   combination in Data Table 1.

Family 2. Father has hemophilia; mother is a carrier of
hemophilia.

Figure 3

Coin 5
Male
Front   Back

6. Place tape on two coins and mark them as shown in Figure 2.

7. Repeat steps 2–5 and tally the combinations in Data Table 2.

Coin 6
Female
Front   Back

Part B: Colorblindness

The allele for red-green colorblindness is also located on the X
chromosome. A female can be $X^C X^C$, $X^C X^c$, or $X^c X^c$. A male can
be either $X^C Y$ or $X^c Y$.

Family 3. Father is colorblind; mother has two dominant
alleles ($X^C X^C$).

Figure 4

Coin 7
Male
Front   Back

1. Place tape on two coins and mark them as shown in Figure 3.

2. Repeat steps 2–5 of Part A and tally the combinations in Data
   Table 3.

Family 4. Parents are not colorblind; mother is heterozygous.

Coin 8
Female
Front   Back

3. Place tape on two coins and mark them as shown in Figure 4.

4. Repeat steps 2–5 of Part A and tally the combinations in Data
   Table 4.

Modern Genetics ▪ *Laboratory Investigation*

How Are Genes on Sex Chromosomes Inherited? *(continued)*

Observations

Data Table 1

Children of $X^H Y$ Father and $X^H X^h$ Mother		
Allele Combination	**Children Observed**	**Total**
$X^H X^H$		
$X^H X^h$		
$X^h X^h$		
$X^H Y$		
$X^h Y$		

Data Table 2

Children of $X^h Y$ Father and $X^H X^h$ Mother		
Allele Combination	**Children Observed**	**Total**
$X^H X^H$		
$X^H X^h$		
$X^h X^h$		
$X^H Y$		
$X^h Y$		

Data Table 3

Children of $X^c Y$ Father and $X^C X^C$ Mother		
Allele Combination	**Children Observed**	**Total**
$X^C X^C$		
$X^C X^c$		
$X^c X^c$		
$X^C Y$		
$X^c Y$		

Modern Genetics · *Laboratory Investigation*

Data Table 4

Children of $X^C Y$ Father and $X^C X^c$ Mother		
Allele Combination	Children Observed	Total
$X^C X^C$		
$X^C X^c$		
$X^c X^c$		
$X^C Y$		
$X^c Y$		

Analyze and Conclude

1. a. How many alleles for hemophilia do females have?

_____

b. How many alleles for red-green colorblindness do females have?

_____

c. How many alleles for hemophilia do males have?

_____

d. How many alleles for red-green colorblindness do males have?

_____

2. Why is there a difference in the number of alleles for hemophilia and red-green colorblindness between males and females?

_____

_____

3. Why are only females carriers for hemophilia? For red-green colorblindness?

_____

_____

_____

4. Which of the parents can pass the allele for hemophilia to a son? Explain.

_____

_____

_____

Modern Genetics · *Laboratory Investigation*

How Are Genes on Sex Chromosomes Inherited? *(continued)*

5. Which of the parents can pass the allele for hemophilia to a daughter? Explain.

_____
_____
_____
_____

6. In Family 3, why are there no colorblind children even though one of the parents is colorblind?

_____
_____
_____
_____

Critical Thinking and Applications

1. The brother of a woman's father has hemophilia. Her father does not have hemophilia, but she is concerned that her son might. Could she have passed the allele for hemophilia to her son? Explain.

_____
_____
_____
_____

2. A woman's father is colorblind. She marries a colorblind man. Might their son be colorblind? Might their daughter be colorblind? Explain.

_____
_____
_____

3. What is the probability that a carrier and a person who has a sex-linked genetic disorder will have a son with the disorder? A daughter? Use your data and a Punnett square to answer these questions.

_____
_____

4. What is the probability that a carrier and a person who does not have a sex-linked genetic disorder will have a son with the disorder? A daughter?

_____
_____

Modern Genetics ▪ *Laboratory Investigation*

More to Explore

Use the Punnett squares to solve the following problems.

1. Two parents have the following alleles for hemophilia: $X^H X^h$ and $X^H Y$.
   What is the probability that a son will have hemophilia? That a daughter
   will have hemophilia?

<table>
<tr><td></td><td></td></tr>
<tr><td></td><td></td></tr>
</table>

_____

_____

2. Two parents have the following alleles for colorblindness: $X^C X^C$ and $X^c Y$.
   What is the probability that a son will be colorblind? A daughter?

<table>
<tr><td></td><td></td></tr>
<tr><td></td><td></td></tr>
</table>

_____

_____

Modern Genetics ▪ *Laboratory Investigation*

How Are Genes on Sex Chromosomes Inherited? *(continued)*

3. Two parents have the following alleles for colorblindness: $X^C X^c$ and $X^C Y$. What is the probability that a son will be colorblind? A daughter?

_____

_____

4. Do your data from the lab support the results from the Punnett squares above? Explain.

_____

_____

_____

_____

Modern Genetics • *Laboratory Investigation*

More to Explore

Use the Punnett squares to solve the following problems.

1. Two parents have the following alleles for hemophilia: $X^H X^h$ and $X^H Y$. What is the probability that a son will have hemophilia? That a daughter will have hemophilia?

_____

_____

2. Two parents have the following alleles for colorblindness: $X^C X^C$ and $X^c Y$. What is the probability that a son will be colorblind? A daughter?

_____

_____

Modern Genetics ▪ *Laboratory Investigation*

How Are Genes on Sex Chromosomes Inherited? *(continued)*

3. Two parents have the following alleles for colorblindness: $X^C X^c$ and $X^C Y$.
   What is the probability that a son will be colorblind? A daughter?

   _____

   _____

4. Do your data from the lab support the results from the Punnett squares
   above? Explain.

   _____

   _____

   _____

   _____

Changes Over Time · *Skills Lab*

Analyze and Conclude

Write your answers in the spaces provided.

1. **Interpreting Data** Which animal's amino acid sequence was most similar to that of the horse? What similarities and difference(s) did you observe?

   _____

   _____

2. **Drawing Conclusions** Based on these data, which species is most closely related to the horse? Which is most distantly related?

   _____

   _____

   _____

3. **Interpreting Data** For the entire protein, the horse's amino acid sequence differs from the other animals' as follows: donkey, 1 difference; rabbit, 6; snake, 22; turtle, 11; and whale, 5. How do the relationships indicated by the entire protein compare with those for the region you examined?

   _____

   _____

4. **Communicating** Write a paragraph explaining why data about amino acid sequences can provide information about evolutionary relationships among organisms.

   _____

   _____

   _____

   _____

   _____

More to Explore

Use the amino acid data to construct a branching tree that includes horses, donkeys, and snakes. The tree should show one way that the three species could have evolved from a common ancestor.

Changes Over Time ▪ *Laboratory Investigation*

Variation in a Population

Pre–Lab Discussion

Are you and your friends all exactly alike? Of course not. Although you are all members of one species, you are different in many ways. These differences are called variations and exist in all species.

Some variations are inherited by the offspring of an organism. Most inherited variations are neutral, that is, they do not affect the organism's survival. Helpful inherited variations are called adaptations. Harmful inherited variations make the organism less suited to its environment. Better-adapted organisms are more likely to reproduce and pass beneficial traits to their offspring. This process is called natural selection.

In this investigation, you will observe variations in two types of plants and in your class population.

1. What does *variations* mean?

_____

_____

2. What variations exist among members of your class?

_____

_____

Problem

How can you measure the variation in plant and animal populations?

Materials *(per group)*

10 large lima beans

10 leaves of the same species

metric ruler

graph paper

3 colored pencils

Safety 🔥 *Review the safety guidelines in Appendix A of your textbook.* Do not eat the lima beans.

Changes Over Time ▪ *Laboratory Investigation*

Procedure

Part A: Variation in Plant Species

1. Obtain 10 large lima beans and 10 leaves of the same species of tree.

2. Measure the length of each lima bean and leaf blade in millimeters. See Figure 1. Record your measurements, rounded to the nearest millimeter, in Data Table 1.

3. Notice in Figure 1 the petiole of the leaf. Measure the length of the petiole of each leaf. Record your measurements, rounded to the nearest millimeter, in Data Table 1.

4. Record on the chalkboard your measurements for each of the plants so that all groups' data can be seen.

5. Using data from the entire class, record the range in lengths for the lima beans, leaf blades, and petioles. Record the class findings in Data Tables 2, 3, and 4. Fill in the first row of each table with the lengths, from shortest to longest, using increments of one millimeter. Add more columns to the data tables if necessary.

6. Record the class's total number of each size of lima bean, leaf blade, and petiole in the second row of Data Tables 2, 3, and 4.

7. Using the data in Data Table 2, construct a line graph for the lima bean lengths on a sheet of graph paper. Label the *x*-axis "Lima bean length (mm)" and the *y*-axis "Number of beans."

8. Using the data in Data Tables 3 and 4, construct line graphs for the leaf-blade lengths and the petiole lengths on your graph paper. Label the *x*-axis "Leaf blade and petiole length (mm)" and the *y*-axis "Number of leaves." Use a different colored pencil to graph each set of data and include a key for each graph.

Blade length

Petiole length

Figure 1

Part B: Variation in Hand Spans

1. Measure your hand span. The measurement should be made from the top of the thumb to the tip of the little finger, as shown in Figure 2. Round off the measurement to the nearest centimeter. Record your hand span in a class chart on the chalkboard.

2. After all your classmates have recorded their hand spans in the class chart, transfer the results to Data Table 5. Your results will show the total number of hands having the same hand span.

3. Construct a line graph of the results on a sheet of graph paper. Label the *x*-axis "Hand-span length (cm)" and the *y*-axis "Number of students."

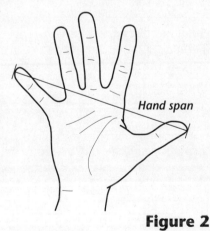

Hand span

Figure 2

Changes Over Time ▪ *Laboratory Investigation*

Variation in a Population (continued)

Observations
Data Table 1

Length (mm) (Group Data)										
	1	**2**	**3**	**4**	**5**	**6**	**7**	**8**	**9**	**10**
Lima beans										
Leaf blades										
Petioles										

Data Table 2

Class Data for Lima Bean Lengths										
Length of lima bean (mm)										
Total number of beans of this size										

Data Table 3

Class Data for Leaf Blade Lengths										
Length of leaf blade (mm)										
Total number of leaf blades of this size										

Data Table 4

Class Data for Petiole Lengths										
Length of petiole (mm)										
Total number of petioles of this size										

Data Table 5

Class Data for Hand-Span Lengths													
Length of hand span (cm)	15	16	17	18	19	20	21	22	23	24	25	26	27	28
Total number of hand spans of this size														

Changes Over Time · *Laboratory Investigation*

Analyze and Conclude

1. In what length range are most of the lima beans? Most of the leaf blades? Most of the petioles?

   _____

2. In what length range are the fewest beans? The fewest blades? The fewest petioles?

   _____

   _____

3. What is the general shape of the graphs of the lengths of the lima beans, leaf blades, and petioles? What does the shape of the graphs indicate about these lengths?

   _____

   _____

   _____

4. Which hand-span length occurs most often? Least often?

   _____

5. What is the general shape of the graph of hand spans? What does the shape of the graph indicate about the hand spans of students in your class?

   _____

   _____

Critical Thinking and Applications

6. List two ways in which a large hand span might be a useful human adaptation.

   _____

   _____

7. Do you think having many seeds in a pod would be a more useful adaptation for a bean plant than having only a few seeds? Give a reason for your answer.

   _____

   _____

8. Why might having large leaves be a harmful characteristic for a desert plant?

   _____

   _____

More to Explore

Investigate variations that occur in the lengths of peanut shells. Make your measurements and graph the results as you did in the previous part of this lab. Do you think that all organisms of the same species show variation in all of their traits? Give a reason for your answer. **CAUTION:** *Do not eat the peanuts.*

Viruses, Bacteria, Protists, and Fungi ▪ *Skills Lab*

How Many Viruses Fit on a Pin?

Problem

How can a model help you understand how small viruses are?

Skills Focus

calculating, making models

Materials

straight pin   long strips of paper   pencil

meter stick   scissors   tape

calculator (optional)

Procedure

1. Examine the head of a straight pin. Write a prediction about the number of viruses that could fit on the pinhead. **CAUTION:** *Avoid pushing the pin against anyone's skin.*

2. Assume that the pinhead has a diameter of about 1 mm. If the pinhead were enlarged 10,000 times, its diameter would measure 10 m. Create a model of the pinhead by cutting and taping together narrow strips of paper to make a strip that is 10 m long. The strip of paper represents the diameter of the enlarged pinhead.

3. Lay the 10-m strip of paper on the floor of your classroom or in the hall. Imagine creating a large circle that had the strip as its diameter. The circle would be the pinhead at the enlarged size. Calculate the area of the enlarged pinhead using this formula:

$$\text{Area} = \pi \times \text{radius}^2$$

   Remember that you can find the radius by dividing the diameter by 2.

4. A virus particle may measure 200 nm on each side (1 nm equals a billionth of a meter). If the virus were enlarged 10,000 times, each side would measure 0.002 m. Cut out a square 0.002 m by 0.002 m to serve as a model for a virus. (*Hint:* 0.002 m = 2 mm.)

5. Next, find the area in meters of one virus particle at the enlarged size. Remember that the area of a square equals side × side.

6. Now divide the area of the pinhead that you calculated in Step 3 by the area of one virus particle to find out how many viruses could fit on the pinhead.

7. Exchange your work with a partner, and check each other's calculations.

Viruses, Bacteria, Protists, and Fungi ▪ *Skills Lab*

Analyze and Conclude

Write your answers on a separate sheet of paper.

1. **Calculating** Approximately how many viruses can fit on the head of a pin?

2. **Predicting** How does your calculation compare with the prediction you made? If the two numbers are very different, explain why your prediction may have been inaccurate.

3. **Making Models** What did you learn about the size of viruses by magnifying both the viruses and pinheads to 10,000 times their actual size?

4. **Communicating** In a paragraph, explain why scientists sometimes make and use enlarged models of very small things, such as viruses.

More to Explore

Think of another everyday object that you could use to model some other facts about viruses, such as their shapes or how they infect cells. Describe your model and explain why the object would be a good choice.

Viruses, Bacteria, Protists, and Fungi • *Skills Lab*

What's for Lunch?

Problem

How does the presence of sugar or salt affect the activity of yeast?

Skills Focus

measuring, inferring, drawing conclusions

Materials

5 small plastic narrow-necked bottles

5 round balloons

5 plastic straws

dry powdered yeast

sugar

salt

warm water (40–45°C)

marking pen

beaker

graduated cylinder

metric ruler

string

Procedure

1. Read over the entire procedure to see how you will test yeast activity in bottles A through E. Write a prediction about what will happen in each bottle.
2. Gently stretch each of the balloons so that they will inflate easily.
3. Using the marking pen, label the bottles *A, B, C, D,* and *E*.
4. Use a beaker to fill each bottle with the same amount of warm water. **CAUTION:** *Glass is fragile. Handle the beaker gently to avoid breakage. Do not touch broken glass.*
5. Put 25 mL of salt into bottle B.

Viruses, Bacteria, Protists, and Fungi ▪ *Skills Lab*

6. Put 25 mL of sugar into bottles C and E.

7. Put 50 mL of sugar into bottle D.

8. Put 6 mL of powdered yeast into bottle A, and stir the mixture with a clean straw. Remove the straw and discard it.

9. Immediately place a balloon over the opening of bottle A. Make sure that the balloon opening fits very tightly around the neck of the bottle.

10. Repeat Steps 8 and 9 for bottle B, bottle C, and bottle D.

11. Place a balloon over bottle E without adding yeast to the bottle.

12. Place the five bottles in a warm spot away from drafts. Every ten minutes for 40 minutes, measure the circumference of each balloon by placing a string around the balloon at its widest part. Include your measurements in the data table.

Viruses, Bacteria, Protists, and Fungi ▪ *Skills Lab*

What's for Lunch? *(continued)*

Data Table						
			Circumference			
Bottle	Prediction	Observations	10 min	20 min	30 min	40 min
A (Yeast alone)						
B (Yeast and 25 mL of salt)						
C (Yeast and 25 mL of sugar)						
D (Yeast and 50 mL of sugar)						
E (No yeast and 25 mL of sugar)						

Analyze and Conclude

Write your answers on a separate sheet of paper.

1. **Measuring** Which balloons changed in size during this lab? How did they change?

2. **Inferring** Explain why the balloon changed size in some bottles and not in others. What caused that change in size?

3. **Interpreting Data** What did the results from bottle C show, compared with the results from bottle D? Why was it important to include bottle E in this investigation?

4. **Drawing Conclusions** Do yeast use salt or sugar as a food source? How do you know?

5. **Communicating** In a paragraph, summarize what you learned about yeast from this investigation. Be sure to support each of your conclusions with the evidence you gathered.

Design an Experiment

Develop a hypothesis about whether temperature affects the activity of yeast cells. Then design an experiment to test your hypothesis. *Obtain your teacher's permission before carrying out your investigation.*

Viruses, Bacteria, Protists, and Fungi ▪ *Laboratory Investigation*

Comparing Protists

Pre-Lab Discussion

Protists are organisms that have nuclei and live in wet environments, such as ponds, oceans, and the bodies of larger organisms. Other than that, protists don't have much in common. For example, some live independently as separate cells; others form colonies of many unattached cells. Plantlike protists are autotrophs—organisms that can make their own food. Animal-like protists and funguslike protists are heterotrophs—organisms that cannot make their own food.

In this investigation, you will observe and compare three common protists: amoebas, euglenas, and paramecia.

1. Protists are eukaryotes. What does that mean?

_____

2. Name three different protist structures that aid in movement.

_____

_____

Problem

How are protists similar? How are they different?

Materials *(per group)*

3 plastic droppers   microscope

amoeba culture   piece of cotton

microscope slide   euglena culture

3 coverslips   paramecium culture

paper towel

Safety  *Review the safety guidelines in Appendix A of your textbook.*

Do not use the same droppers for different cultures. Always use both hands to pick up or carry a microscope. Hold the microscope base with one hand and hold the microscope arm with your other hand. Handle glass slides carefully. Don't handle broken glass. Wash your hands thoroughly after the lab.

Procedure

1. With a plastic dropper, place a drop of the amoeba culture on the slide.

2. Make a wet-mount slide by gently laying the coverslip over the drop of amoeba culture.

Viruses, Bacteria, Protists, and Fungi ▪ *Laboratory Investigation*

Comparing Protists *(continued)*

3. Touch a piece of paper towel to the edge of the coverslip to blot up any excess liquid. See Figure 1.

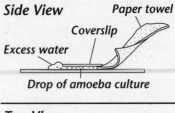

Side View   Paper towel
Coverslip
Excess water
Drop of amoeba culture

4. Place the slide on the stage of the microscope. Use the low-power objective to bring an amoeba into focus. Have the teacher check to see that you have an amoeba in focus.

5. Switch to the high-power objective. **CAUTION:** *When turning to the high-power objective, always look at the objective from the side of your microscope. Don't let the objective hit the slide.*

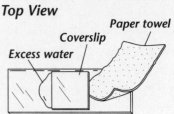

Top View   Paper towel
Coverslip
Excess water

6. Use the fine-adjustment knob to bring the organism into sharper focus. **CAUTION:** *Never focus the high-power objective with the coarse-adjustment knob. The objective could break the slide.*

7. Observe an amoeba and draw what you see in Plate 1 in Observations. Label the nucleus, cell membrane, cytoplasm, food vacuole, and pseudopods. Record the microscope magnification that you used below your sketch.

8. Carefully clean and dry the slide with a paper towel.

9. Separate a few strands of cotton and place them on the slide. The cotton strands will help slow down the euglena. Using a clean dropper, add a drop of the euglena culture to the strands of cotton.

10. Repeat steps 2–6 with the drop of euglena culture.

11. Observe a euglena and draw what you see in Plate 2 in Observations. Label the nucleus, cell membrane, cytoplasm, eyespot, flagellum, and chloroplasts. Record the microscope magnification you used below your sketch.

12. Carefully clean and dry the slide.

13. Separate a few strands of cotton and place them on the slide. Using a clean dropper, add a drop of the paramecium culture to the strands of cotton.

14. Repeat steps 2–6 with the drop of paramecium culture.

15. Observe a paramecium and draw what you see in Plate 3 in Observations. Label the cytoplasm, cell membrane, cilia, nucleus, contractile vacuole, food vacuoles, oral groove, and gullet. Record the microscope magnification you used below your sketch.

16. Clean and dry the slide once again. Return all the materials to the teacher. Wash your hands when you're finished with the lab.

Observations

1. Describe the shape of the amoeba.

_____

2. Describe the shape of the euglena.

_____

Viruses, Bacteria, Protists, and Fungi · *Laboratory Investigation*

3. Describe the shape of the paramecium.

   _____

4. Describe how an amoeba moves.

   _____

5. Describe how a euglena moves.

   _____

6. Describe how a paramecium moves.

   _____

7. What structures does the euglena have that the amoeba and paramecium do not have?

   _____

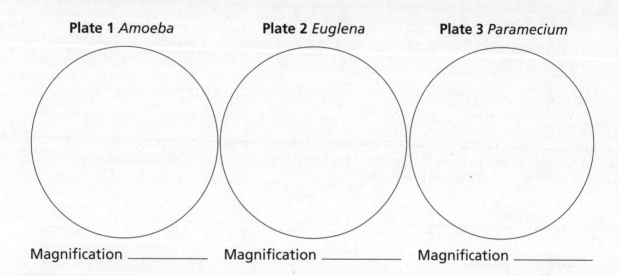

Plate 1 *Amoeba*   **Plate 2** *Euglena*   **Plate 3** *Paramecium*

Magnification _____   Magnification _____   Magnification _____

Analyze and Conclude

1. What structures do all the protists have?

   _____

2. Which protist has structures that are characteristic of both autotrophs and heterotrophs?

   _____

3. Classify the three protists that you observed as animal-like, funguslike, or plantlike protists. Give a reason for your answers.

   _____

   _____

   _____

Viruses, Bacteria, Protists, and Fungi • *Laboratory Investigation*

Comparing Protists *(continued)*

4. Which is the slowest moving of the three protists?

_____

5. Why are some protists able to move faster than others?

_____

_____

Critical Thinking and Applications

1. Why is the eyespot an important structure in the euglena?

_____

_____

2. The paramecium has two types of cilia. One type covers its entire surface. The other is at the entrance to the gullet. How does the paramecium use each type?

_____

_____

_____

3. Certain cells in your body, such as white blood cells, move by amoeboid motion. What does this mean?

_____

_____

More to Explore

A paramecium has thousands of cilia that project through the pellicle—the covering that gives the paramecium its shape. These cilia beat with a wavelike pattern that keeps a paramecium moving smoothly in one direction. Write a hypothesis for how a paramecium will respond when it runs into objects that are in its path. Write a procedure you would follow to test your hypothesis. Have the teacher approve your procedure before you carry out the investigation. Describe how the paramecium responds. Did your results support your hypothesis?

Plants · *Skills Lab*

Masses of Mosses

Problem

How is a moss plant adapted to carry out its life activities?

Skills Focus

observing, measuring

Materials

clump of moss
metric ruler
plastic dropper
hand lens
toothpicks
water

Procedure

1. Your teacher will give you a clump of moss. Examine the clump from all sides. Draw a diagram of what you see. Measure the size of the overall clump and the main parts of the clump. Record your observations.

2. Using toothpicks, gently separate five individual moss plants from the clump. Be sure to pull them totally apart so that you can observe each plant separately. If the moss plants appear to dry up as you are working, moisten them with a few drops of water.

Plants ▪ *Skills Lab*

Masses of Mosses *(continued)*

3. Measure the length of the leaflike, stemlike, and rootlike structures on each plant. If brown stalks and capsules are present, measure them. Find the average length of each structure.

4. Make a drawing of a single moss plant. Label the parts, give their sizes, and record the color of each part. When you are finished observing the moss, return it to your teacher. Wash your hands thoroughly.

5. Obtain class averages for the sizes of the structures you measured in Step 3. Also, if the moss that you observed had brown stalks and capsules, share your observations about those structures.

Analyze and Conclude

Write your answers on a separate sheet of paper.

1. **Observing** Describe the overall appearance of the moss clump, including its color, size, and texture.

2. **Measuring** What was the typical size of the leaflike portion of the moss plants, the typical height of the stemlike portion, and the typical length of the rootlike portion?

3. **Inferring** In which part(s) of the moss does photosynthesis occur? How do you know?

4. **Communicating** Write a paragraph explaining what you learned about mosses from this investigation. Include explanations of why mosses cannot grow tall and why they live in moist environments.

More to Explore

Select a moss plant with stalks and capsules. Use toothpicks to release some of the spores, which can be as small as dust particles. Examine the spores under a microscope. Create a labeled drawing of what you see.

Plants · *Skills Lab*

A Close Look at Flowers

Problem

What is the function of a flower, and what roles do its different parts play?

Skills Focus

observing, inferring, measuring

Materials

paper towels	large flower	water
plastic dropper	coverslip	metric ruler
hand lens	scalpel	lens paper
microscope	tape	
slide		

Procedure

PART 1 The Outer Parts of the Flower

1. Tape four paper towel sheets on your work area. Obtain a flower from your teacher. While handling the flower gently, observe its shape and color. Use the ruler to measure it. Notice whether the petals have any spots or other markings. Does the flower have a scent? Record your observations with sketches and descriptions.

2. Observe the sepals. How many are there? How do they relate to the rest of the flower? (*Hint:* Sepals are often green, but not always.) Record your observations.

3. Use a scalpel to carefully cut off the sepals without damaging the structures beneath them. **CAUTION:** *Scalpels are sharp. Cut in a direction away from yourself and others.*

4. Observe the petals. How many are there? Are all the petals the same, or are they different? Record your observations.

Plants · *Skills Lab*

A Close Look at Flowers *(continued)*

PART 2 The Male Part of the Flower

5. Carefully pull off the petals to examine the male part of the flower. Try not to damage the structures beneath the petals.

6. Observe the stamens. How many are there? How are they shaped? How tall are they? Record your observations.

7. Use a scalpel to carefully cut the stamens away from the rest of the flower without damaging the structures beneath them. Lay the stamens on the paper towel.

8. Obtain a clean slide and coverslip. Hold a stamen over the slide, and gently tap some pollen grains from the anther onto the slide. Add a drop of water to the pollen. Then place the coverslip over the water and pollen.

9. Observe the pollen under both the low-power objective and the high-power objective of a microscope. Draw and label a pollen grain.

PART 3 The Female Part of the Flower

10. Use a scalpel to cut the pistil away from the rest of the flower. Measure the height of the pistil. Examine its shape. Observe the top of the pistil. Determine if that surface will stick to and lift a tiny piece of lens paper. Record your observations.

11. Lay the pistil on the paper towel. Holding it firmly at its base, use a scalpel to cut the pistil in half at its widest point, as shown in the diagram below. **CAUTION:** *Cut away from your fingers.* How many compartments do you see? How many ovules do you see? Record your observations.

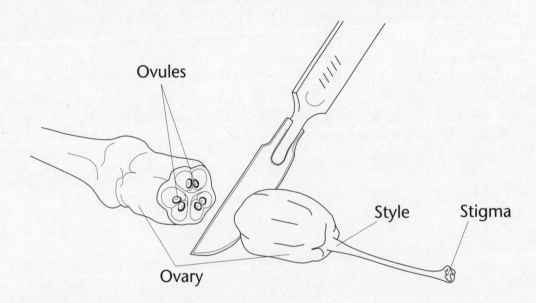

Plants · *Skills Lab*

Analyze and Conclude

Write your answers on a separate sheet of paper.

1. **Observing** Based on your observations, describe how the sepals, petals, stamens, and pistils of a flower are arranged.

2. **Inferring** How are the sepals, petals, stamens, and pistil involved in the function of this flower?

3. **Measuring** Based on your measurements of the heights of the pistil and stamens, how do you think the flower you examined is pollinated? Use additional observations to support your answer.

4. **Classifying** Did you find any patterns in the number of sepals, petals, stamens, or other structures? If so, describe that pattern. Is your flower a monocot or a dicot?

5. **Communicating** Write a paragraph explaining all you can learn about a plant by examining one of its flowers. Use your observations in this lab to support your conclusions.

More to Explore

Some kinds of flowers do not have all the parts found in the flower used in this lab. Obtain a different flower. Find out which parts this flower has, and which parts are missing. *Obtain your teacher's approval before carrying out this investigation.*

Investigating Stomata

Pre-Lab Discussion

For an organism to live and grow naturally in any place, it must be adapted to the conditions of that place. A land plant, for example, must have adaptations that prevent it from drying out. A thick, waxy layer of tissue, called the cuticle, is one adaptation that prevents water loss. However, the cuticle also prevents exchange of oxygen and carbon dioxide with the environment. Photosynthesis cannot take place without this exchange of gases. Small openings, called stomata (singular *stoma*), allow gases to move into and out of the plant. Each stoma is surrounded by two guard cells that control the size of the opening. When these guard cells absorb water, the stoma opens; when the guard cells lose water, the stoma closes.

In this investigation, you will observe stomata in a land plant and in a floating water plant.

1. Why is photosynthesis important for plants?

_____

_____

_____

2. What adaptations make it possible for plants to live on land?

_____

_____

_____

Problem

How do the number and position of stomata differ in plants from different environments?

Materials *(per group)*

leaf from a land plant

leaf from a floating water plant

scissors

microscope

2 slides

dropper

2 coverslips

Name _____ Date _____ Class _____

Plants · *Laboratory Investigation*

Safety   *Review the safety guidelines in Appendix A of your textbook.*

Use caution in handling sharp scissors. Handle glass slides carefully. Do not let the microscope lens touch the slide.

Procedure

1. Predict where stomata are on the leaf of a land plant. Give a reason for your prediction.

   _____

   _____

2. Select a land plant. With the lower epidermis (underside of the leaf) facing upward, bend and then tear the leaf at an angle as illustrated below. This will reveal part of the thin, colorless, lower epidermis.

Step 1

Step 2

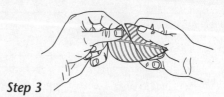

Step 3

3. With the scissors, cut off a strip of the colorless tissue and make a wet-mount slide. Place the slide on the microscope stage and focus under low power. Locate the stomata. Switch to high power. Draw the stomata, the guard cells, and a few of the lower epidermis cells in Observations. Count the stomata seen in the field of vision under high power. Record your data in the Data Table. (Identify and record the name of your lab group in the first column of the Data Table. Record data only in the row for your group.)

4. Repeat Step 3, using the upper epidermis of the same leaf. Draw your observations. Count the stomata seen in the field of vision under high power and record your data.

5. Predict where stomata are on the leaf of a floating water plant. Give a reason for your prediction.

   _____

   _____

6. Repeat Step 3, using the lower epidermis of a leaf from a water plant. Draw what you see in Observations. Count the stomata in the field of vision and record this number in the Data Table.

7. Repeat Step 3, using the upper epidermis of a leaf from the water plant. Draw your observations and record your data.

8. Exchange and record data from other groups to complete your Data Table.

Plants ▪ *Laboratory Investigation*

Investigating Stomata *(continued)*

Observations

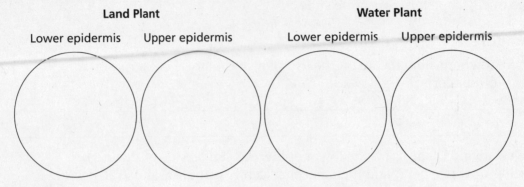

Land Plant

Lower epidermis   Upper epidermis

Water Plant

Lower epidermis   Upper epidermis

Data Table

| Group | Land Plant: _____ | | Floating Water Plant: _____ | |
	Lower Epidermis	Upper Epidermis	Lower Epidermis	Upper Epidermis

Analyze and Conclude

1. Is the class information more reliable than the information gathered by one group? Give a reason for your answer.

   _____

2. Using data from the entire class, compare the number of stomata in the upper and lower epidermis of land plants.

   _____

3. Using data from the entire class, compare the number of stomata in the upper and lower epidermis of water plants.

   _____

Plants · *Laboratory Investigation*

Critical Thinking and Applications

1. What advantage could the number of stomata and their location provide for land plants?

_____

_____

_____

2. What advantage could the number of stomata and their location provide for floating water plants?

_____

_____

3. When do you think stomata are usually open—during the day or at night? Give a reason for your answer.

_____

_____

4. How could you change the procedure you followed to improve the accuracy of the data?

_____

_____

More to Explore

New Problem Are stomata affected by a salt solution?

Possible Materials Consider which materials you can use from the previous part of the lab. What other materials might you need?

Procedure Develop a procedure to solve the problem. Keep in mind that in osmosis, water moves from an area where it is concentrated to an area where it is less concentrated. Write your procedure on a separate sheet of paper. Have the teacher approve your procedure before you carry out the investigation.

Observations Keep records of your observations on a separate sheet of paper.

Analyze and Conclude Were more stomata open or closed in the salt solution? What might explain your results?

_____

_____

_____

Sponges, Cnidarians, and Worms • *Consumer Lab*

Soak It Up!

Problem

Which sponge absorbs the most water?

Skills Focus

observing, predicting, communicating

Materials

damp piece of cellulose sponge
damp piece of natural sponge
damp piece of foam sponge
balance
large bowl of tap water
graduated cylinder
beaker
paper towel

Procedure

1. Fill in the data table below as you work through the procedure.

Data Table				
			Volume of Absorbed Water	
Type of Sponge	**Mass of Damp Sponge**	**Size of Pores**	**Total (mL)**	**Per Gram (mL/g)**
Cellulose				
Natural				
Foam				

2. Examine the size of the pores in each sponge. Record your observations in the data table.

3. Make a prediction about which sponge will absorb the most water. Record your prediction and give a reason.

_____

_____

Sponges, Cnidarians, and Worms • *Consumer Lab*

4. Place a damp piece of cellulose sponge on a balance and measure its mass. Record the mass in the data table. Remove the sponge from the balance.

5. Repeat Step 4 with the natural sponge and then the foam sponge.

6. Submerge the cellulose sponge in a bowl of water. Squeeze it several times to remove all air bubbles. Release the sponge and let it absorb water. Then remove the sponge and place it in the beaker.

7. Squeeze out as much water as possible from the sponge into the beaker. (*HINT:* Squeeze and twist the sponge until no more drops of water come out.)

8. Pour the water from the beaker into the graduated cylinder. Measure the volume of water and record the volume in the data table. Pour the water from the graduated cylinder back into the bowl. Dry the graduated cylinder and beaker with a paper towel.

9. Repeat Steps 6–8 using the natural sponge and then the foam sponge. When you are finished, squeeze all the water from your sponges, and return them to your teacher.

10. Calculate the volume of water absorbed per gram of each type of sponge, using this formula:

$$\frac{\text{Volume of absorbed water}}{\text{Mass of damp sponge}} = \text{Volume absorbed per gram}$$

Analyze and Conclude

1. **Observing** Which sponge absorbed the most water per gram of sponge? The least? Was your prediction confirmed?

2. **Drawing Conclusions** What can you conclude about the relationship between pore size and the ability of the sponge to absorb water?

3. **Predicting** How would the volume of absorbed water change if each of the sponges had twice the mass of the sponges you studied? Explain.

4. **Communicating** Natural sponges can cost more than cellulose and foam sponges. Consider that information and the results of your investigation. Which sponge would you recommend to consumers for absorbing water spills? Explain your choice.

Design an Experiment

Design an experiment to test the prediction you made in Question 3 above. Write your hypothesis as an "If … then …" statement. *Obtain your teacher's permission before carrying out your investigation.*

Name _____ Date _____ Class _____

Earthworm Responses

Problem

Do earthworms prefer dry or moist environments? Do they prefer light or dark conditions?

Skills Focus

observing, interpreting data

Materials

plastic dropper
water
cardboard
clock or watch
paper towels
flashlight
2 earthworms
storage container
tray

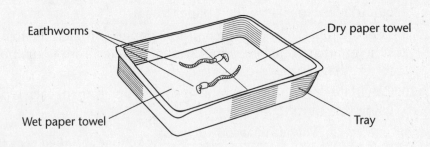

Earthworms — Dry paper towel

Wet paper towel — Tray

Procedure

1. Which environment do you think earthworms prefer—dry or moist? Record your hypothesis in the space below.

   _____

   _____

   _____

2. Use the dropper to sprinkle water on the worms. Keep the worms moist at all times.

3. Fold a dry paper towel and place it on the bottom of one side of your tray. Fold a moistened paper towel and place it on the other side.

4. Moisten your hands. Then place the earthworms in the center of the tray. Make sure that half of each earthworm's body rests on the moist paper towel and half rests on the dry towel. Handle the worms gently.

5. Cover the tray with the piece of cardboard. After five minutes, remove the cardboard and observe whether the worms are on the moist or dry surface. Record your observations in the space below.

   _____

   _____

   _____

Sponges, Cnidarians, and Worms • *Skills Lab*

6. Repeat Steps 4 and 5. Record your observations in the space below.

_____

_____

_____

7. Return the earthworms to their storage container. Moisten the earthworms with water.

8. Which do you think earthworms prefer—strong light or darkness? Record your hypothesis in the space below.

_____

_____

_____

9. Cover the whole surface of the tray with a moistened paper towel.

10. Place the earthworms in the center of the tray. Cover half of the tray with cardboard. Shine a flashlight onto the other half.

11. After five minutes, note the locations of the worms. Record your observations in the space below.

_____

_____

_____

12. Repeat Steps 10 and 11. Record your observations in the space below.

_____

_____

_____

13. Moisten the earthworms and put them in the location designated by your teacher. Wash your hands after handling the worms.

Sponges, Cnidarians, and Worms · *Skills Lab*

Earthworm Responses *(continued)*

Analyze and Conclude

Write your answers on a separate sheet of paper.

1. **Observing** Which environment did the worms prefer—moist or dry? Bright or dark?

2. **Interpreting Data** Did the worms' behavior support your hypotheses?

3. **Communicating** Explain in a paragraph what knowledge or experiences helped you develop your hypotheses at the beginning of the experiments.

Design an Experiment

Do earthworms prefer a smooth or rough surface? Write your hypothesis. Then design an experiment to answer the question. *Obtain your teacher's permission before carrying out your investigation.*

Sponges, Cnidarians, and Worms • *Laboratory Investigation*

Observing Flatworms and Roundworms

Pre-Lab Discussion

Flatworms have flat bodies and a body cavity with one opening. Many are parasites, living inside or on other organisms. Although most free-living flatworms live in the oceans, some live in fresh water or in soil.

Roundworms have long, cylindrical bodies that taper to a point at each end. There are more species of roundworms than any other kind of worm. They live in nearly every kind of moist environment, including forest soils, Antarctic sand, and pools of super-hot water. Like flatworms, some roundworms are parasitic and others are free-living.

In this investigation, you will observe some of the characteristics of parasitic and free-living flatworms and roundworms.

1. What are the three main groups of worms?

_____

_____

2. Why are some kinds of tapeworms of concern to dog owners?

_____

_____

Problem

What are some characteristics of flatworms and roundworms?

Materials *(per group)*

microscope
planarian slide
pork-tapeworm slide
vinegar-eel slide
trichina-worm slide

Safety   *Review the safety guidelines in Appendix A of your textbook.*

Procedure

Part A: Observing Flatworms

1. CAUTION: *Handle the slides carefully; they're breakable.* Use a microscope to look at a planarian slide under low magnification. Planarians are free-living, freshwater flatworms that have a definite head with a simple brain. Locate the two eyespots in the head region. They sense light. Find the mouth in the middle of the body on the ventral (belly) surface. Note a long tube, the pharynx, through which food moves from the mouth into the gastrovascular cavity. The gastrovascular cavity digests food and circulates it to the entire body. It also gets rid of waste.

Sponges, Cnidarians, and Worms · *Laboratory Investigation*

Observing Flatworms and Roundworms (continued)

2. Sketch a planarian under low power in the appropriate space in Observations. Label the eyespots, mouth, pharynx, and gastrovascular cavity. Record the magnification you used next to your sketch.

3. Tapeworms live as parasites inside the bodies of other animals. They attach themselves to the inner walls of their hosts and take in food through their skin. Examine a slide of a tapeworm under low magnification. Find the head. Note several suckers and the ring of hooks on the head. Behind the head is a narrow neck. The rest of the tapeworm's body is a string of nearly square sections that grow from the neck. The youngest sections are closest to the neck. These sections contain the male and female reproductive organs.

4. Sketch the tapeworm under low power in the appropriate space in Observations. Label the head, suckers, hooks, neck, young sections, and older sections. Record the magnification you used next to your sketch.

Part B: Observing Roundworms

1. A vinegar eel is a roundworm usually found in vinegar. Examine a slide of a vinegar eel under low magnification. Find the mouth at its anterior (head) end and the anus at its posterior (tail) end. Note the bulblike pharynx and long intestine. If the vinegar eel is female, eggs will be lined up in the uterus. If it is male, it will have a single testis.

2. Sketch the vinegar eel under low power in the appropriate space in Observations. Label the mouth, pharynx, intestine, anus, eggs (if female), and testis (if male). Record the magnification you used next to your sketch.

3. Examine a slide of a trichina worm. This worm is often found inside a hard capsule called a cyst. Such cysts are located inside the muscle tissue of the host.

4. Sketch what you see in the appropriate space in Observations. Label the trichina worm, cyst, and muscle tissue. Record the magnification you used next to your sketch.

Name _____ Date _____ Class _____

Sponges, Cnidarians, and Worms • *Laboratory Investigation*

Observations

Planarian

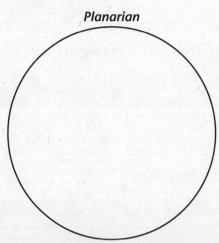

Magnification: _____

Tapeworm

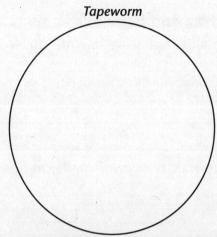

Magnification: _____

Vinegar eel (male)

Magnification: _____

Vinegar eel (female)

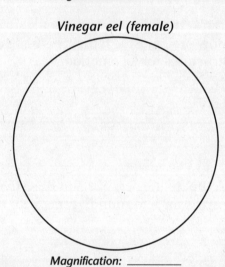

Magnification: _____

Trichina worm in muscle tissue

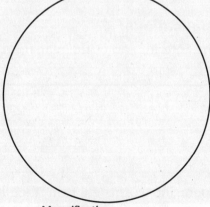

Magnification: _____

Sponges, Cnidarians, and Worms • *Laboratory Investigation*

Observing Flatworms and Roundworms *(continued)*

Analyze and Conclude

1. Identify two ways in which flatworms and roundworms differ in body structure.

_____

_____

_____

_____

2. How are flatworms similar to roundworms in body structure?

_____

_____

_____

_____

3. How are parasitic flatworms and roundworms able to survive without structures for locomotion?

_____

_____

_____

_____

4. Compare the nervous and digestive systems of the free-living forms of flatworms and roundworms with those of parasitic forms.

_____

_____

_____

_____

Critical Thinking and Applications

1. Why is the structure at the anterior end of the planarian body called an eyespot instead of an eye?

_____

_____

_____

2. List two necessities that parasitic worms get from their hosts that free-living worms have to obtain for themselves.

_____

_____

_____

Sponges, Cnidarians, and Worms ▪ *Laboratory Investigation*

3. Why is it rare that an individual parasite kills its host?

_____

_____

_____

_____

_____

4. You have a new job as a product inspector in a large meat-packing company. Your first assignment is to inspect pork for trichina worms. You've been warned that if humans eat undercooked or raw pork that has a large number of trichina worms in it, a serious infection can result. What should you look for?

_____

_____

_____

_____

Sponges, Cnidarians, and Worms ▪ *Laboratory Investigation*

Observing Flatworms and Roundworms *(continued)*

More to Explore

New Problem Do planarians prefer to live in a light environment or a dark one?

Possible Materials List materials that you will be using in this experiment.

Safety Keep planarians in pond water at all times, so they will not be harmed. Always treat animals with great care. Use both hands to carry a microscope. Hold the microscope base with one hand and the microscope arm with your other hand. Handle glass slides carefully. Wash your hands after completing the investigation.

Procedure Hypothesize whether planarians prefer to live in a light environment or a dark one. On a separate sheet of paper, write a procedure you would follow to test your hypothesis. Have the teacher approve your procedure before you carry out the investigation.

Observations Make appropriate data tables and drawings.

Analyze and Conclude

1. Was your hypothesis supported by your data? Why or why not?

_____

_____

_____

_____

_____

2. Based on your experiment, what can you infer about where planarians live in nature?

_____

_____

_____

_____

_____

Mollusks, Arthropods, and Echinoderms • *Skills Lab*

A Snail's Pace

Problem

How do changes in the temperature of the environment affect the activity level of a snail?

Skills Focus

interpreting data, predicting

Materials

freshwater snail

thermometer

ruler

plastic petri dish

graph paper, 2 sheets

timer

spring water at three temperatures: cool (9–13°C); medium (18–22°C); warm (27–31°C)

Procedure

1. Use the data table on the next page to record your data.

2. On one sheet of graph paper labeled *Snail,* trace a circle using the base of an empty petri dish. Divide and label the circle as shown in the illustration. On a second sheet of graph paper labeled *Data,* draw three more circles like the one in the illustration.

3. Place the petri dish over the circle on the Snail page, fill it with cool water, and record the water temperature. Then place the snail in the water just above the "S" in the circle. Be sure to handle the snail gently.

Mollusks, Arthropods, and Echinoderms • *Skills Lab*

A Snail's Pace (continued)

4. For five minutes, observe the snail. Record its movements by drawing a line that shows its path in the first circle on the Data page.

5. Find the distance the snail moved by measuring the line you drew. You may need to measure all the parts of the line and add them together. Record the distance in your data table.

6. Repeat Steps 3 through 5, first with medium-temperature water and then with warm water. Record the snail's paths in the second circle and third circle on the Data page.

7. Return the snail to your teacher when you are done. Wash your hands thoroughly.

8. For each temperature, compute the class average for distance traveled.

Data Table

	Cool	Medium	Warm
Water Temperature			
Distance			

Analyze and Conclude

Write your answers on a separate sheet of paper.

1. **Graphing** Make a bar graph showing the class average for each temperature.

2. **Interpreting Data** How does a snail's activity level change as temperature increases?

3. **Predicting** Do you think the pattern you found would continue at higher temperatures? Explain.

4. **Communicating** Write an e-mail to a friend describing how you conducted your experiment, any problems you ran into, and your results. Did your results help answer the question posed at the beginning of the lab? Explain your results to your friend.

Design an Experiment

Design an experiment to measure how different kinds of natural surfaces beneath the snail affect its rate of movement. Obtain three surface materials, such as fine sand, medium-grain gravel, and coarse gravel. Explain how you would modify the procedure. *Obtain your teacher's permission before carrying out your investigation.*

Mollusks, Arthropods, and Echinoderms • *Skills Lab*

What's Living in the Soil?

Problem

What kinds of animals live in soil and leaf litter?

Skills Focus

observing, classifying

Materials

2-liter plastic bottle
large scissors
trowel
cheesecloth
large rubber band
gooseneck lamp
hand lens
large, wide-mouthed jar
small jar
coarse steel wool
fresh sample of soil and leaf litter

Procedure

1. Select a location where your equipment can be set up and remain undisturbed for about 24 hours. At that location, place the small jar inside the center of the large jar.

2. Use scissors to cut a large plastic bottle in half. **CAUTION:** *Cut in a direction away from yourself and others.* Turn the top half of the bottle upside down to serve as a funnel.

3. Insert a small amount of coarse steel wool into the mouth of the funnel to keep the soil from falling out. Do not pack the steel wool too tightly. Leave spaces for small organisms to crawl through. Place the funnel into the large jar.

4. Using the trowel, fill the funnel with soil and surface leaf litter. When you finish, wash your hands thoroughly.

5. Look closely to see whether the soil and litter are dry or wet. Record your observation.

Mollusks, Arthropods, and Echinoderms · *Skills Lab*

What's Living in the Soil? *(continued)*

6. Make a cover for your sample by placing a piece of cheesecloth over the top of the funnel. Hold the cheesecloth in place with a large rubber band. Immediately position a lamp about 15 cm above the funnel, and turn on the light. Allow this setup to remain undisturbed for about 24 hours. **CAUTION:** *Hot light bulbs can cause burns. Do not touch the bulb.*

7. When you are ready to make your observations, turn off the lamp. Leave the funnel and jar in place while making your observations. Use a hand lens to examine each organism in the jar. **CAUTION:** *Do not touch any of the organisms.*

8. Use the data table below to sketch each type of organism and to record other observations. Be sure to include evidence that will help you classify the organisms. (*Hint:* Remember that some animals may be at different stages of metamorphosis.)

9. Examine the soil and leaf litter, and record whether this material is dry or wet.

10. When you are finished, follow your teacher's directions about returning the organisms to the soil. Wash your hands with soap.

Data Table

Sketch of Organism	Number Found	Size	Important Characteristics	Probable Phylum

Mollusks, Arthropods, and Echinoderms ▪ *Skills Lab*

Sketch of Organism	Number Found	Size	Important Characteristics	Probable Phylum

Analyze and Conclude

Write your answers on a separate sheet of paper.

1. **Observing** Describe the conditions of the soil environment at the beginning and end of the lab. What caused the change?
2. **Classifying** What types of animals did you collect in the small jar? What characteristics did you use to identify each type of animal? Which types of animals were the most common?
3. **Developing Hypotheses** Why do you think the animals moved down the funnel away from the soil?
4. **Inferring** Using what you have learned about arthropods and other animals, make an inference about the role that each animal you collected plays in the environment.
5. **Communicating** Develop a field guide that categorizes and describes the types of animals you found in your soil sample. Include sketches and brief descriptions of the animals.

Design an Experiment

What kinds of organisms might live in other soil types—for example, soil at the edge of a pond, dry sandy soil, or commercially prepared potting soil? Design an experiment to answer this question.

Mollusks, Arthropods, and Echinoderms • *Laboratory Investigation*

Characteristics of Sea Stars

Pre-Lab Discussion

The sea star, or starfish, is a spiny-skinned sea invertebrate in the echinoderm phylum. Echinoderms are animals whose bodies are usually covered with hundreds of small spines. Brittle stars, basket stars, sand dollars, sea cucumbers, and sea urchins are also echinoderms.

Sea stars live in coastal waters and on rocky seashores. They are predators that eat oysters, clams, snails, barnacles, and worms. Sea stars usually have five arms branching out from a central disk. Sun stars have seven to 14 arms, however, and some sea stars have 15 to 24 arms. If an arm breaks off, the sea star can regenerate the arm, meaning it can grow a new one.

In this investigation, you will examine the external structures of a sea star.

1. The name *echinoderm* means "spiny skinned." Is this a good name for this phylum? Explain.

   _____

   _____

   _____

2. What characteristics are typical of echinoderms?

   _____

   _____

Problem

How is the anatomy of a sea star adapted to sea life?

Materials *(per group)*

wet paper towels
preserved sea star
dissecting tray
2 hand lenses

Safety   *Review the safety guidelines in Appendix A of your textbook.*
To prevent skin irritation, wear an apron and goggles during this investigation.

Mollusks, Arthropods, and Echinoderms · *Laboratory Investigation*

Procedure

1. Put on safety goggles and a lab apron. **CAUTION:** *The preservative used on the sea star can irritate your skin. Don't touch your eyes or mouth while working with the preserved sea star. Keep a piece of wet paper towel handy to wipe your fingers after touching the star.* Rinse the sea star thoroughly with water to remove any extra preservative. Put the sea star, top surface up, in the dissecting tray. Notice that the sea star's body has five arms radiating from a central disk.

2. Using a hand lens, examine the skin on the top surface. Notice the many coarse spines that cover the entire top surface. The skin is spiny and irregular because parts of the endoskeleton protrude through the skin. Around the base of the spines are jawlike structures. They capture small animals and keep the skin free of foreign objects.

3. Use a hand lens to locate a spine and the jawlike structures around it. See Figure 1. Answer Observations question 1.

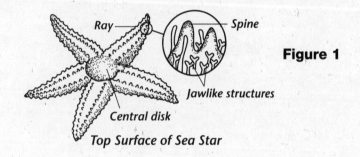

Ray — Spine

Figure 1

Jawlike structures

Central disk

Top Surface of Sea Star

4. Study the top surface of the central disk. Answer Observations question 2.

5. Locate a small red or yellow buttonlike structure on the top side of the central disk. This structure contains many tiny pores through which water enters the water vascular system. The water vascular system has water-filled canals that function primarily in movement and feeding.

6. Try to find the anus on the top surface of the central disk. The anus, which opens out from the intestine, lets solid wastes escape from the body.

7. In Observations, label the following structures on the top side of the sea star: central disk, arms, spines, and anus.

8. Turn the sea star over so that its bottom surface is visible. With the hand lens, examine the mouth, an opening in the middle of the central disk. Notice the small spines that surround the mouth. Many types of sea stars feed by pushing part of the stomach through the mouth. The stomach secretes enzymes that digest prey.

9. Find the grooves that begin at the mouth and extend down the center of each arm. Find the small tube feet that line the grooves. The tube feet are part of the water vascular system. A tube foot is a hollow, thin-walled cylinder with a bulblike structure at one end and a sucker at the tip. Answer Observations question 3.

Mollusks, Arthropods, and Echinoderms • *Laboratory Investigation*

Characteristics of Sea Stars *(continued)*

10. In Observations, label the following structures on the bottom side of the sea star: groove, mouth, and tube feet.

11. When you have finished examining the specimen, follow the teacher's instructions for storing the sea star for further use. **CAUTION:** *Wash your hands thoroughly at the end of the lab.*

Observations

Top Side of Sea Star

Bottom Side of Sea Star

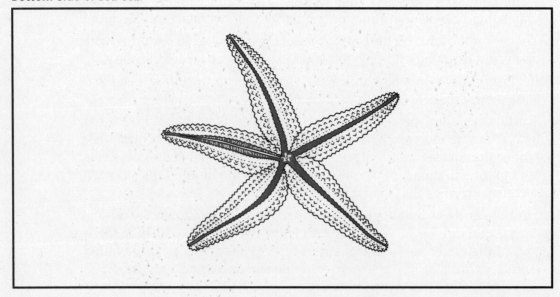

Name _____ Date _____ Class _____

Mollusks, Arthropods, and Echinoderms • *Laboratory Investigation*

1. Describe the appearance of a sea star's spines.

   _____

   _____

2. How does the number of spines in the central disk compare to the number of spines in the arm?

   _____

   _____

3. How many rows of tube feet does your sea star have?

   _____

   _____

Analyze and Conclude

1. What do you think the function of a sea star's spines might be?

   _____

   _____

2. What kind of symmetry does a sea star have?

   _____

   _____

3. What do you think the tube feet might be used for?

   _____

   _____

4. How do you think a sea star might eat?

   _____

   _____

   _____

   _____

5. What internal structures enable the sea star to capture food and to move? Explain how the structures do this.

   _____

   _____

   _____

   _____

Mollusks, Arthropods, and Echinoderms • *Laboratory Investigation*

Characteristics of Sea Stars *(continued)*

Critical Thinking and Applications

1. Sea stars produce large numbers of eggs and sperm. Why is this production an advantage?

   _____

   _____

   _____

   _____

2. When a sea star pries open the shell of a clam or an oyster, the mollusk resists. Even if the shell opens only slightly, the sea star will get its meal. How does this happen?

   _____

   _____

   _____

   _____

   _____

3. Because sea stars eat many clams and oysters, divers were hired to catch sea stars, chop them into pieces, and throw them back into the ocean. After this, fishers found even more empty clam and oyster shells than before. Why did their plan backfire?

   _____

   _____

   _____

   _____

4. Can a sea star move equally well in any direction? Why or why not?

   _____

   _____

   _____

5. Many echinoderms, which are bottom dwellers as adults, have free-swimming larvae. What advantages do free-swimming larvae have?

   _____

   _____

   _____

   _____

Mollusks, Arthropods, and Echinoderms • *Laboratory Investigation*

More to Explore

New Problem Why do sand dollars, sea urchins, sea lilies, sea cucumbers, and brittle stars belong to the same phylum as sea stars?

Possible Materials List and gather the materials you will need. Decide which materials you could use from the previous lab.

Safety Wear aprons and goggles if working with specimens.

Procedure Write a hypothesis that includes those features that you think each of these organisms share. Write a procedure you would follow to test your hypothesis. Have the teacher approve your procedure before you carry out the investigation.

Observations Make drawings and record other observations on a separate sheet of paper.

Analyze and Conclude What characteristics do your observed animals share that place them in the same phylum as sea stars?

_____

_____

_____

Fishes, Amphibians, and Reptiles · *Skills Lab*

Soaking Up Those Rays

Problem

How do some lizards control their body temperatures in the extreme heat of a desert?

Skills Focus

Interpreting data, predicting

Materials

paper   pencil

Procedure

1. The data below were collected by scientists studying how lizards control their body temperature. Examine the data.

2. Fill in the data table below as you work through the procedure.

3. Organize the data in the diagrams by filling in the table, putting the appropriate information in each column. Begin by writing a brief description of each type of lizard behavior.

4. Complete the data table using the information in the diagrams.

6 A.M.–7 A.M.
Emerging from burrow
Air temperature **20°C**
Ground temperature **28°C**
Body temperature **25°C**

7 A.M.–9 A.M.
Basking (lying on ground in sun)
Air temperature **27°C**
Ground temperature **29°C**
Body temperature **32.6°C**

9 A.M.–12 Noon
Active (moving about)
Air temperature **27°C**
Ground temperature **30.8°C**
Body temperature **36.6°C**

12 Noon–2:30 P.M.
Retreat to burrow
Air temperature **40.3°C**
Ground temperature **53.8°C**
Body temperature **39.5°C**

2:30 P.M.–6 P.M.
Stilting (belly off ground)
Air temperature **34.2°C**
Ground temperature **47.4°C**
Body temperature **39.5°C**

6 P.M.–9 P.M.
Retreat to burrow
Air temperature **25°C**
Ground temperature **26°C**
Body temperature **25°C**

Fishes, Amphibians, and Reptiles • *Skills Lab*

		Data Table			
Activity	Description of Activity	Time of Day	Air Temp. (°C)	Ground Temp. (°C)	Body Temp. (°C)
1. Emerging					
2. Basking					
3. Active					
4. Retreat					
5. Stilting					
6. Retreat					

Analyze and Conclude

Answer the following questions on a separate sheet of paper.

1. **Interpreting Data** Describe how the lizard's body temperature changed between 6 A.M. and 9 P.M.

2. **Inferring** What are three sources of heat that caused the lizard's body temperature to rise during the day?

3. **Interpreting Data** During the hottest part of the day, what were the air and ground temperatures? Why do you think the lizard's temperature remained below 40°C?

4. **Predicting** Predict what the lizard's body temperature would have been from 9 P.M. to 6 A.M. Explain your prediction.

5. **Predicting** Predict what would happen to your own body temperature if you spent a brief period outdoors in the desert at noon. Predict what your temperature would be if you spent time in a burrow at 7 P.M. Explain your predictions.

6. **Drawing Conclusions** Based on what you learned from the data, explain why it is misleading to say that an ectotherm is a "coldblooded" animal.

7. **Communicating** Write a paragraph explaining why it is helpful to organize data in a data table before you try to interpret the data.

More to Explore

Make a bar graph of the temperature data. Explain what the graph shows you. How does this graph help you interpret the data about how lizards control their body temperature in the extreme heat of a desert?

Fishes, Amphibians, and Reptiles · *Skills Lab*

Home Sweet Home

Problem

What features does an aquarium need for fish to survive in it?

Skills Focus

observing, making models

Materials

gravel
metric ruler
guppies
snails
guppy food
dip net
tap water
thermometer
water plants
aquarium filter
aquarium heater
rectangular aquarium tank
    (15 to 20 liters) with cover

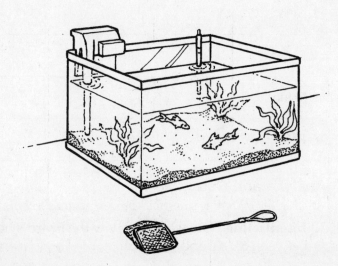

Procedure

1. Wash the aquarium tank with lukewarm water—do not use soap. Then place it on a flat surface in indirect sunlight.

2. Rinse the gravel and spread it over the bottom of the tank to a depth of about 3 cm.

3. Fill the tank about two-thirds full with tap water. Position several water plants in the tank by gently pushing their roots into the gravel. Wash your hands after handling the plants.

4. Add more water until the level is about 5 cm from the top.

5. Place the filter in the water and turn it on. Insert an aquarium heater into the tank and turn it on. Set the temperature to 25°C. **CAUTION:** *Do not touch electrical equipment with wet hands.*

6. Allow the water to "age" by letting it stand for 2 days. Aging allows chlorine to evaporate.

Fishes, Amphibians, and Reptiles • *Skills Lab*

7. When the water has aged and is at the proper temperature, add guppies and snails to the tank. Include one guppy and one snail for each 4 liters of water. Cover the aquarium. Wash your hands after handling the animals.

8. Observe the aquarium every day for 2 weeks. Feed the guppies a small amount of food daily. Look for evidence that the fishes and snails have adapted to their new environment. Also look for the ways they carry out their life activities, such as feeding and respiration. Record your observations on a separate sheet of paper.

9. Use a dip net to keep the gravel layer clean and to remove any dead plants or animals.

Analyze and Conclude

Answer the following questions on a separate sheet of paper.

1. **Observing** How does the aquarium meet the following needs of the organisms living in it: (a) oxygen supply, (b) proper temperature, and (c) food?

2. **Inferring** What happens to the oxygen that the fish take in from the water in this aquarium? How is that oxygen replaced?

3. **Making Models** How is an aquarium like a guppy's natural environment? How is it different?

4. **Communicating** Write an e-mail to a friend or relative in which you summarize the record you made during the two weeks you observed the aquarium.

Design an Experiment

Write a one-page procedure for adding a second kind of fish to the aquarium. Include a list of questions that you would need to have answered before you could carry out your plan successfully. (Success would be marked by both types of fishes surviving together in the tank.) *Obtain your teacher's permission before carrying out your investigation.*

Fishes, Amphibians, and Reptiles ▪ *Laboratory Investigation*

Adaptations of Fishes

Pre-Lab Discussion

Fishes are vertebrate members of the phylum Chordata. The largest group of fishes has skeletons made of bones. The perch and the goldfish are bony fishes. Bony fishes exhibit many adaptations for life in water. All fishes are ectotherms. They live in water and have fins. Fins are fanlike structures used for steering, balancing, and moving. Most fishes obtain oxygen through gills and have scales. Scales are thin, hard, overlapping plates that cover the skin of fish.

In this investigation, you will observe the movement and behavior of a live goldfish. You will also identify the external parts of a perch.

1. Explain how a fish obtains oxygen.

_____

_____

2. What are the three major groups of fishes? Describe their characteristics.

_____

_____

_____

Problem

How are the structures of fishes adapted for life in water?

Materials *(per group)*

large glass jar or beaker
water from an aquarium (to fill beaker)
fishnet
goldfish
paper towels
preserved perch
dissecting tray
probe
forceps
hand lens
microscope slide
medicine dropper
coverslip

Fishes, Amphibians, and Reptiles · *Laboratory Investigation*

Safety 📋 🧪 🧤 🧪 ⚗️ ☠️ 🔥 🐭 *Review the safety guidelines in Appendix A of your textbook.*

Always treat living things with great care. Keep the goldfish in the aquarium water as much as possible. Do not use tap water directly from the tap. Tap water must be left at room temperature for at least 24 hours before placing fish in it. To prevent slips or falls, immediately wipe up any water spilled on the floor. To prevent skin irritation, wear aprons and goggles during Part B. Handle glass items carefully. Tell your teacher about any broken glass.

Procedure

Part A: Observing the Behavior of a Live Fish

1. Fill a large glass or beaker three-quarters full with water from an aquarium.

2. **CAUTION:** *Keep the goldfish in the water as much as possible.* With a fishnet, carefully remove one goldfish from the aquarium. Immediately transfer the fish to the jar of water.

3. Observe the goldfish. Find the gills. Carefully watch the movements of the body, fins, and tail as the goldfish swims. Answer Observations question 1.

4. Use the labeled diagram of the perch to find the goldfish's dorsal, caudal, pectoral, pelvic, and anal fins. Answer Observations question 2. Observe the function of each fin as the fish swims. Complete the Data Table on fins.

5. With a fishnet, carefully return the goldfish to the aquarium.

Part B: Examining the External Anatomy of a Fish

1. Put on safety goggles and a lab apron. **CAUTION:** *The preservative used on the perch can irritate your skin. Don't touch your eyes or mouth while working with the fish. Keep a piece of wet paper towel handy to wipe your fingers after touching the fish.* Rinse the perch thoroughly with water to remove any extra preservative. Dry the fish with paper towels. Position the fish in a dissecting tray with the head of the fish pointing left.

2. Observe the dorsal (back) and ventral (belly) surfaces. Answer Observations question 3.

3. Find the three regions of the fish's body: the head, the trunk, and the tail.

4. Find the nostril—one of two openings between the eye and the mouth.

5. Insert a probe into the mouth and carefully pry it open. Observe the teeth. **CAUTION:** *Do not touch the fish's teeth; they are very sharp.* Answer Observations question 4.

6. With a probe, carefully lift the protective bony cover away from the gills lying underneath. Observe the flat, scalelike bones that support the gill cover.

Fishes, Amphibians, and Reptiles • *Laboratory Investigation*

Adaptations of Fishes *(continued)*

7. With forceps, carefully remove a single scale. Observe the scale with a hand lens. Notice the growth rings. As a fish grows, its scales grow. Each growth ring on the scale represents one year's growth. Answer Observations question 5. In Observations, draw a scale as seen under the hand lens. Label the growth rings on your drawing.

8. On the diagram in Observations, label the following parts of the external anatomy of a perch: head, trunk, tail, eye, nostril, mouth, upper jaw, lower jaw, gills, and scales.

9. When you have finished examining the fish, follow your teacher's instructions for storing the perch for further use. **CAUTION:** *Wash your hands thoroughly at the end of the lab.*

Observations

Data Table	
Fin on Goldfish	**Function** *Choose from among the following:* • *Helps fish steer and stop* • *Keeps fish from rolling over* • *Propels fish through water* • *No apparent function*
Anterior dorsal (on back near head)	
Posterior dorsal (on back near tail)	
Anal	
Caudal	
Pectoral	
Pelvic	

Perch Scale

On a separate sheet of paper, make a drawing of a perch scale as seen under the hand lens. Label the growth rings.

Name _____ Date _____ Class _____

Fishes, Amphibians, and Reptiles • *Laboratory Investigation*

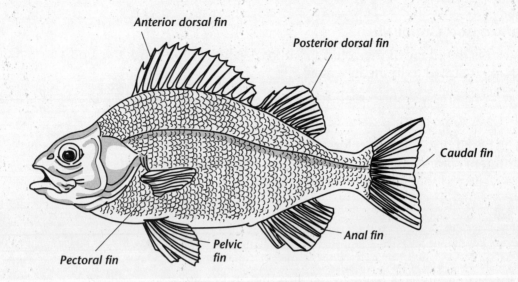

Anterior dorsal fin

Posterior dorsal fin

Caudal fin

Anal fin

Pelvic fin

Pectoral fin

1. Describe the motion of the goldfish as it swims.
   _____
   _____

2. How many fins does the goldfish have? Which fins occur in pairs?
   _____
   _____

3. Compare the color of the dorsal and ventral surfaces of the perch.
   _____
   _____
   _____

4. Describe the perch's teeth. Where are they in the mouth?
   _____
   _____

5. How old is your perch?
   _____
   _____

Fishes, Amphibians, and Reptiles · *Laboratory Investigation*

Adaptations of Fishes *(continued)*

Analyze and Conclude

1. What is the shape of the goldfish's body? Why do you think this body shape is suited to living in water?

   _____

   _____

2. The perch has different colors on its back and belly. How do these different colors protect the fish from its enemies, both the birds in the sky above it and the sea organisms that live below it?

   _____

   _____

   _____

3. How are the perch's teeth adapted to their function?

   _____

   _____

4. What structures on the perch make it adapted for life in water?

   _____

   _____

Critical Thinking and Applications

1. While many invertebrates have an exoskeleton, or hard shell covering, vertebrates such as fishes have an endoskeleton. How does the endoskeleton help the fishes?

   _____

   _____

2. The perch has a gas-filled internal structure called a swim bladder. What is the function of the swim bladder?

   _____

   _____

   _____

   _____

Fishes, Amphibians, and Reptiles · *Laboratory Investigation*

3. Certain species of fishes that live deep in the ocean have chemicals in their skin that make them glow in the dark. How does this characteristic help these fishes survive in their environment?

_____

_____

_____

4. The perch fertilizes its eggs externally and leaves them exposed on underwater rocks. The guppy fertilizes its eggs internally and gives birth to live young. Which fish probably produces fewer eggs? Which species is likely to have a higher survival rate for its young?

_____

_____

_____

_____

_____

_____

More to Explore

What does a fish skeleton look like? Obtain a fish from a grocery store. Boil the fish so that the flesh peels off easily. Or, if you prefer, cook the fish for dinner and carefully remove the meat so that the skeleton remains intact. Sketch and label the fish's skeleton.

Birds and Mammals · *Skills Lab*

Looking at an Owl's Leftovers

Problem

What can you learn about owls' diets from studying the pellets that they cough up?

Skills Focus

observing, drawing conclusions

Materials

owl pellet

hand lens

dissecting needle

metric ruler

forceps

Procedure

1. An owl pellet is a collection of undigested materials that an owl coughs up after a meal. Write a hypothesis describing what items you expect an owl pellet to contain. List the reasons for your hypothesis.

2. Use a hand lens to observe the outside of an owl pellet. Record your observations.

3. Use one hand to grasp the owl pellet with forceps. Hold a dissecting needle in your other hand, and use it to gently separate the pellet into pieces. **CAUTION:** *Dissecting needles are sharp. Never cut material toward you; always cut away from your body.*

4. Using the forceps and dissecting needle, carefully separate the bones from the rest of the pellet. Remove any fur that might be attached to bones.

5. Group similar bones together in separate piles. Observe the skulls, and draw them. Record the number of skulls, their length, and the number, shape, and color of the teeth.

6. Use the chart on the next page to determine what kinds of skulls you found. If any skulls do not match the chart exactly, record which animal skulls they resemble most.

7. Try to fit together any of the remaining bones to form complete or partial skeletons. Sketch your results.

8. Wash your hands thoroughly with soap when you are finished.

Birds and Mammals · *Skills Lab*

Shrew	Upper jaw has at least 18 teeth; tips of the teeth are reddish brown. Skull length is 23 mm or less.
House mouse	Upper jaw has two biting teeth and extends past lower jaw. Skull length is 22 mm or less.
Meadow Vole	Upper jaw has two biting teeth that are smooth, not grooved. Skull length is 23 mm or more.
Mole	Upper jaw has at least 18 teeth. Skull length is 23 mm or more.
Rat	Upper jaw has two biting teeth. Upper jaw extends past lower jaw. Skull length is 22 mm or more.

Record your observations on a separate sheet of paper.

Birds and Mammals ▪ *Skills Lab*

Looking at an Owl's Leftovers *(continued)*

Analyze and Conclude

Write your answers on a separate sheet of paper.

1. **Observing** How many animals' remains were in the pellet? What observations led you to that conclusion?
2. **Drawing Conclusions** Combine your results with those of your classmates. Which three animals were eaten most frequently? How do these results compare to your hypothesis?
3. **Calculating** Owls cough up about two pellets a day. Based on your class's data, what can you conclude about the number of animals an owl might eat in one month?
4. **Communicating** In this lab, you were able to examine only the part of the owl's diet that it did not digest. In a paragraph, explain how this fact might affect your confidence in the conclusions you reached.

Design an Experiment

Design a study that might tell you how an owl's diet varies at different times of the year. Give an example of a hypothesis you could test with such an experiment. What variables would you control? Before carrying out your experiment, obtain your teacher's approval of your plan.

Birds and Mammals · *Consumer Lab*

Keeping Warm

Problem

Do wool products provide insulation from the cold? How well does wool insulate when it is wet?

Skills Focus

graphing, interpreting data

Materials

tap water, hot

scissors

beaker, 1-L

3 thermometers

clock or watch

graph paper

a pair of wool socks

tap water, room temperature

3 containers, 250-mL, with lids

Procedure

1. Put one container into a dry woolen sock. Soak a second sock with water at room temperature, wring it out so it's not dripping, and then slide the second container into the wet sock. Both containers should stand upright. Leave the third container uncovered.

2. Use scissors to carefully cut a small "X" in the center of each lid, making the X just large enough for a thermometer to pass through.

3. Fill a beaker with about 800 mL of hot tap water. Then pour hot water nearly to the top of each of the three containers. **CAUTION:** *Avoid spilling hot water on yourself or others.*

4. Place a lid on each of the containers, and insert a thermometer into the water through the hole in each lid. Gather the socks around the thermometers above the first two containers so that the containers are completely covered.

5. Immediately measure the temperature of the water in each container, and record it in the data table on the next page. Take temperature readings every 5 minutes for at least 15 minutes.

Birds and Mammals ▪ *Consumer Lab*

Keeping Warm (continued)

Data Table

	Starting Temperature	5-Minute Temperature	10-Minute Temperature	15-Minute Temperature
Dry Sock Container				
Wet Sock Container				
No Sock Container				

Analyze and Conclude

Answer the following questions on a separate sheet of paper.

1. **Graphing** Graph your results using a different color to represent each container. Graph time in minutes on the horizontal axis and temperature on the vertical axis.

2. **Interpreting Data** Compare the temperature changes in the three containers. Relate your findings to the insulation characteristics of mammal skin coverings.

3. **Communicating** Suppose a manufacturer claims that its wool socks will keep your feet warm even if they get wet. Do your findings support this claim? Write a letter to the company explaining why or why not.

Design an Experiment

Design an experiment to compare how wool's insulating properties compare with those of other natural materials (such as cotton) or manufactured materials (such as acrylic). *Obtain your teacher's permission before carrying out your investigation.*

Birds and Mammals ▪ *Laboratory Investigation*

Adaptations of Birds

Pre-Lab Discussion

Whether you are in an open meadow, a city park, or your own backyard, you are likely to hear the sounds of birds. There are many different bird species, and each has special adaptations to its environment. For example, birds can have different types of feathers. These feathers, which are actually modified scales, provide insulation and balance. Birds also have bills or beaks of various shapes and sizes. The shapes of bills are adaptations to the different kind of foods found in the birds' environment.

The feet of birds are also adapted to specific environments. In addition to walking and running, birds' feet are used for gripping and tearing food, climbing, and swimming. The shape and size of the feet determine how well a bird can perform these tasks within its specific environment.

In this investigation, you will examine how birds' bills and feet help them survive in their environment.

1. What are some types of food that birds eat?

   _____

   _____

2. In addition to eating, what are other functions of birds' bills?

   _____

   _____

Problem

How have birds adapted to living in different environments?

Materials *(per class)*

- 30 petri dishes
- 4 bags of different seeds or seedlike materials, such as sunflower seeds, popcorn, lima beans, or couscous
- 6 different hand tools
- clock or watch with a second hand

Safety   *Review the safety guidelines in Appendix A of your textbook.*

Use caution in handling pointed or sharp tools. Keep seeds in containers at all times to prevent spills and accidents. Do not eat seeds. Wash hands after handling seeds.

Birds and Mammals ▪ *Laboratory Investigation*

Adaptations of Birds *(continued)*

Procedure

Part A: Modeling Bills

1. **CAUTION:** *Handle pointed or sharp tools carefully.* There are several stations around your classroom. At each station you will find the following: a tool; four petri dishes, each filled with a different type of seed; and an empty petri dish. The tools will be used to model the effectiveness of different bill shapes in picking up seeds. Each station has a different tool-bill. Visit each station briefly and examine the different tool-bills and seeds.

2. Predict which tool-bill will work best to pick up each type of seed. Give a reason for your prediction.

   Seed 1 _____

   Seed 2 _____

   Seed 3 _____

   Seed 4 _____

   Predict which tool-bill will be the worst at picking up each type of seed. Give a reason for your prediction.

   Seed 1 _____

   Seed 2 _____

   Seed 3 _____

   Seed 4 _____

3. Go to one station and practice using the tool-bill to pick up the different seeds. Pick up one seed at a time. Each petri dish contains only one type of seed. Be sure not to mix the seeds in the petri dishes. Use either one or both hands to hold the tool-bill. Everyone in the group should practice using the tool-bill.

4. While a classmate times you, use the tool-bill to pick up as many seeds from the Seed 1 dish as you can within 30 seconds. Pick up only one seed at a time and place it into the empty petri dish. Count how many seeds you pick up within 30 seconds and record this number in Data Table 1 on the next page. When your time is up, return the seeds to the Seed 1 dish. Everyone in the group should take a turn at picking up as many seeds as possible from the Seed 1 dish.

Birds and Mammals ▪ *Laboratory Investigation*

5. Repeat Step 4 for the other three types of seeds at the station. Calculate the average number of seeds picked up by your group within 30 seconds for each type of seed. Record the averages in your data table.

6. Repeat steps 3–5 at each station. Record your data in Date Table 1.

Observations

Part A

Data Table 1: Number of Seeds Picked up in 30 Seconds

Station Number _____   Tool _____

Student Name	Seed 1	Seed 2	Seed 3	Seed 4
1.				
2.				
3.				
4.				
Average Number of Seeds				

Station Number _____   Tool _____

Student Name	Seed 1	Seed 2	Seed 3	Seed 4
1.				
2.				
3.				
4.				
Average Number of Seeds				

Station Number _____   Tool _____

Student Name	Seed 1	Seed 2	Seed 3	Seed 4
1.				
2.				
3.				
4.				
Average Number of Seeds				

Name _____ Date _____ Class _____

Birds and Mammals · *Laboratory Investigation*

Adaptations of Birds (continued)

Station Number _____ Tool _____

Student Name	Seed 1	Seed 2	Seed 3	Seed 4
1.				
2.				
3.				
4.				
Average Number of Seeds				

Station Number _____ Tool _____

Student Name	Seed 1	Seed 2	Seed 3	Seed 4
1.				
2.				
3.				
4.				
Average Number of Seeds				

Station Number _____ Tool _____

Student Name	Seed 1	Seed 2	Seed 3	Seed 4
1.				
2.				
3.				
4.				
Average Number of Seeds				

Birds and Mammals ▪ *Laboratory Investigation*

1. List the tool-bills in order of effectiveness at picking up each type of seed.
   Begin with the most effective tool and end with the least effective.

   Seed 1 _____

   Seed 2 _____

   Seed 3 _____

   Seed 4 _____

2. Were some tool-bills more effective at picking up a certain type of seed
   than other tool-bills? Name the tool-bills and which seeds they picked up
   more effectively.

   _____

   _____

   _____

3. Were some tool-bills effective at picking up a variety of seeds? If so, name them.

   _____

   _____

Part B: Examining Bird Beaks and Feet

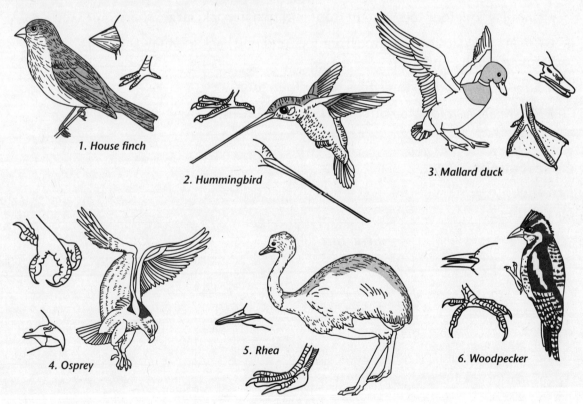

1. House finch

2. Hummingbird

3. Mallard duck

4. Osprey

5. Rhea

6. Woodpecker

Figure 1

Birds and Mammals · *Laboratory Investigation*

Adaptation of Birds *(continued)*

Procedure

Part B: Examining Bird Beaks and Feet

1. Examine and compare the shape and size of each bird's bill in Figure 1. Use the following list to infer the likely structure and function of the bill for each bird. Record this information in Data Table 2.

   - *Straight and pointed:* used as a chisel to drill trees

   - *Flat and broad:* used to strain algae and small organisms from water

   - *Massive and hooked:* used to tear flesh

   - *Short and stout:* multipurpose; used to eat insects, seeds, and small crustaceans

   - *Long, fine, pipelike tube:* used to obtain nectar from flowers

2. Examine and compare the feet of the birds in Figure 1. Use the following list to determine the number and position (front or back of the foot) of the toes and to infer the function of the feet for each bird. Record this information in Data Table 3 on the following page.

   - *Climbing foot:* four toes; two toes in front and two toes in back for support when climbing upward to prevent falling backward

   - *Grasping foot:* four toes; two in front and two in back; large, sharp curved claws

   - *Perching foot:* four toes; three front toes and one back toe that can hold onto a perch tightly

   - *Running foot:* two to three toes rather than four

   - *Swimming foot:* four toes; three in front and one in back; webbed feet that act as paddles

Observations

Part B

Data Table 2

Bird	Structure of Bill	Function of Bill
1. House finch		
2. Hummingbird		
3. Mallard duck		
4. Osprey		
5. Rhea		
6. Woodpecker		

Birds and Mammals · *Laboratory Investigation*

Data Table 3

Bird	Number of Toes	Toe Positions	Function
1. House finch			
2. Hummingbird			
3. Mallard duck			
4. Osprey			
5. Rhea			
6. Woodpecker			

Analyze and Conclude

1. How do your results for the tool-bills compare with your predictions? Give possible reasons for differences.

   _____

   _____

2. Based on the information you have gathered, describe what a bill that can effectively pick up and crack small seeds might look like.

   _____

   _____

3. If a bird has grasping feet and a large hooked bill, what might the bird eat? Explain your answer.

   _____

   _____

Critical Thinking and Applications

1. Why would a woodpecker probably be unsuccessful if it were to depend on small mammals for food?

   _____

   _____

2. What advantage might a bird that is able to eat a variety of seeds have over a bird that can eat only one type of seed?

   _____

   _____

Birds and Mammals ▪ *Laboratory Investigation*

Adaptation of Birds (continued)

3. A bird has been sighted in a mountainous area, where it lives at high altitudes and low temperatures. There are few, if any, trees and food sources are limited. Only sagebrush and some grass grow up through the mostly snow-covered land. Most likely, the bird would spend a lot of time on the ground, as does the ptarmigan, with three toes in front and a large toe in back for balance. What might a bird in this environment eat? What might its beak and feet look like? Explain your answer.

_____

_____

_____

_____

More to Explore

Using the information below and the previous activity, draw the beaks and feet of the following birds in the spaces provided. If you like, use your imagination to draw the whole bird as well. To the left of each illustration, explain your drawing.

Bird A lives in a South American tropical forest and eats nuts, seeds, and fruit. This bird makes nests in holes in trees and has been seen gathering on a cliff of salty clay to lick minerals.

Bird B is a songbird that sits in the trees of India and Malaysia. This bird eats flower nectar as well as insects. Sometimes it hovers before tube-shaped flowers and reaches into them with its long tongue. But when it feeds from large blooms, it pierces the petals to reach the nectar at the base.

Animal Behavior · *Design Your Own Lab*

Become a Learning Detective

Problem

What are some factors that make it easier for people to learn new things?

Skills Focus

calculating, posing questions, designing experiments

Suggested Materials

paper and pencil

Design a Plan

List A	List B
zop	bug
rud	rag
tig	den
wab	hot
hev	fur
paf	wax
mel	beg
kib	cut
col	sip
nug	job

1. Look over the two lists of words in the table. Researchers use groups of words like these to investigate how people learn. Notice the way the two groups differ. The words in List A have no meanings in ordinary English. List B contains familiar but unrelated words.

2. What do you think will happen if people try to learn the words in each list? Write a hypothesis about which list will be easier to learn. How much easier will it be to learn that list?

3. With a partner, design an experiment to test your hypothesis. Brainstorm a list of the variables you will need to control in order to make your results reliable. Then write out your plan and present it to your teacher.

4. If necessary, revise your plan according to your teacher's instructions. Then perform your experiment using people your teacher has approved as test subjects. Keep careful records of your results.

Name _____ Date _____ Class _____

Animal Behavior ▪ *Design Your Own Lab*

Data Table

List A	zop	rud	tig	wab	hev	paf	mel	kib	col	nug	Total

List B	bug	rag	den	hot	fur	wax	beg	cut	sip	job	Total

Analyze and Conclude

Write your answers on a separate sheet of paper.

1. **Calculating** Find the average (mean) number of words people learned from each list. How do the results compare with your hypothesis?

2. **Posing Questions** What factors may have made one list easier to learn than the other? What other questions can you ask about your data?

3. **Designing Experiments** Look back at your experimental plan. Think about how well you were able to carry it out in the actual experiment. What difficulties did you encounter? What improvements could you make, either in your plan or in the way you carried it out?

4. **Communicating** Share your results with the rest of the class. How do the results of the different experiments in your class compare? What factors might explain the similarities or differences?

More to Explore

Plan an experiment to investigate how long people remember what they learn. Develop a hypothesis, and design an experiment to test your hypothesis.

Animal Behavior · *Skills Lab*

One for All

Problem

How does an ant society show organization and cooperative behavior?

Skills Focus

observing, developing hypotheses

Materials

large glass jar	sponge	black paper
sandy soil	20–30 ants	tape
shallow pan	hand lens	glass-marking pencil
water	bread crumbs	forceps
wire screen	sugar	large, thick rubber band

Procedure

1. Read over the entire lab to preview the kinds of observations you will be making.

2. Mark the outside of a large jar with four evenly spaced vertical lines. Label the sections with the letters A, B, C, and D. You can use these labels to identify the sections of soil on and below the surface.

3. Fill the jar about three-fourths full with soil. Place the jar in a shallow pan of water to prevent any ants from escaping. Place a wet sponge on the surface of the soil as a water source for the ants.

4. Observe the condition of the soil, both on the surface and along the sides of the jar. Record your observations.

5. Add the ants to the jar. Immediately cover the jar with the wire screen, using the rubber band to hold the screen firmly in place.

6. Observe the ants for at least 10 minutes. Look for differences in the appearance of adult ants, and look for eggs, larvae, and pupae. Examine both individual behavior and interactions between the ants.

Animal Behavior • *Skills Lab*

One for All *(continued)*

7. Remove the screen cover and add small amounts of bread crumbs and sugar to the soil surface. Close the cover. Observe the ants for at least 10 minutes.

8. Create dark conditions for the ants by covering the jar with black paper above the water line. Remove the paper only when you are making your observations.

9. Observe the ant colony every day for two weeks. Remove the dark paper, and make and record your observations. Look at the soil as well as the ants, and always examine the food. If any food has started to mold, use forceps to remove it. Place the moldy food in a plastic bag, seal the bag, and throw it away. Add more food as necessary, and keep the sponge moist. When you finish your observations, replace the dark paper.

10. At the end of the lab, follow your teacher's directions for returning the ants.

Data Table				
Date	Section A	Section B	Section C	Section D

Animal Behavior · *Skills Lab*

Analyze and Conclude

Answer the following questions on a separate sheet of paper.

1. **Observing** Describe the various types of ants you observed. What differences, if any, did you observe in their behavior? What evidence did you see of different kinds of ants performing different tasks?

2. **Inferring** How do the different behaviors you observed contribute to the survival of the colony?

3. **Inferring** How did the soil change over the period of your observations? What caused those changes? How do you know?

4. **Communicating** What kinds of environmental conditions do you think ant colonies need to thrive outdoors? Use the evidence you obtained in this lab to write a paragraph that supports your answer.

Design an Experiment

Design an experiment to investigate how an ant colony responds when there is a change in the ants' environment, such as the introduction of a new type of food. *Obtain your teacher's permission before carrying out your investigation.*

Animal Behavior • *Laboratory Investigation*

Family Life of Bettas

Pre-Lab Discussion

Betta fish, also known as Siamese fighting fish, live in fresh water and originally came from Southeast Asia. These beautiful aquarium fish are usually red, blue, or turquoise. The males' colors become brighter when the fish are courting or get excited. Bettas do not get all their oxygen from water; they rise to the surface from time to time for air. They can live in containers without special pumps or filters.

In this investigation, you will select a male and a female betta fish, set them up in a container, and observe them to see if they will produce a batch of eggs that will hatch into tiny fish, called fry. During your investigation, remember that fish, like all other living organisms, must be handled with care. The containers that you will be using must be filled with tap water that has been sitting for at least 24 hours. The water should be changed once a week. Floating aquatic plants must be present when both male and female bettas are in the same container. The fish prefer low light, and the water should be kept between 21°C and 29°C (70°F and 84°F). Betta fish should be fed a pinch of food twice a day. Male bettas are extremely territorial and MUST be kept out of sight of one another.

1. What type of behavior is courtship—instinctive or learned? Explain your answer.

   _____

   _____

2. Betta males are very aggressive toward one another. What is aggressive behavior?

   _____

   _____

Problem

What behaviors enable betta fish to reproduce?

Animal Behavior • *Laboratory Investigation*

Materials *(per group)*

colored pencils

2 clean 2-liter soda bottles filled with aged water

1-gallon or larger container filled with aged water

aquarium gravel

floating clump of aquatic plants

betta food

male and female betta fish

hand lens

Safety *Review the safety guidelines in Appendix A of your textbook.* Wash your hands after handling the fish.

Procedure

1. Read the entire lab before continuing your investigation.

2. Brainstorm with other students on how to use the materials to set up a container for your fish to live in. Have the teacher approve your plans before you set up these containers with your fish.

3. Place your male and female bettas in separate containers for one or two days. Sketch the fish in Observations and record their behaviors in the Data Table. Observations may include periods of inactivity, gill movements, how the fish swims, and which fins it uses in different maneuvers. Note differences in the sexes, gill movements, and fin and tail formation.

4. After one or two days, introduce both fish into a larger breeding container. Observe your fish for 10 minutes every day, for up to two weeks. Watch for the events listed below. You may not see every event take place. Compare your observations with those of your classmates. Record all of the fish's behaviors each day and answer the questions in Observations.

   ■ initial reaction of the male and female bettas after being introduced into the same container

   ■ initial courtship behaviors

   ■ male building nest (between 24 hours and 5 days after introduction to female)

   ■ female approaching male and laying eggs

   ■ care of eggs

   ■ hatching of eggs into fry (Eggs hatch within 24 to 28 hours of being laid.) Use a hand lens to check the eggs in the water. Fry are very small and may be difficult to see without magnification.

   ■ care of fry by adults

Animal Behavior · *Laboratory Investigation*

Family Life of Bettas (continued)

5. When your observations are complete, plan with the teacher how to continue to care for the fish.

Observations

Sketch of Male and Female Fish

Male betta   Female betta

1. After placing the male and female fish into the same container, what happens to the bodies of the male and female fish when they first notice each other?

   _____

   _____

2. What types of courtship behaviors do the fish show?

   _____

   _____

   _____

3. While the male betta is building the nest, how do the behaviors of the two fish change?

   _____

   _____

   _____

   _____

   _____

4. What behavior occurs before the eggs are laid and while the eggs are being laid?

   _____

   _____

   _____

   _____

   _____

Animal Behavior · *Laboratory Investigation*

5. How do the adult bettas take care of the nest, eggs, and fry?

_____

_____

_____

_____

Data Table

Day	Behavior Observations	
	Male	Female
1–2; fish in separate containers		
3; fish are put into one container		

Animal Behavior · *Laboratory Investigation*

Family Life of Bettas *(continued)*

Analyze and Conclude

1. Did your bettas successfully reproduce? If not, suggest some possible reasons the pair did not breed.

_____

_____

_____

_____

2. Why are the courtship behaviors of the male and female bettas important?

_____

_____

_____

_____

Critical Thinking and Applications

1. Why are the floating plants important to the female betta?

_____

_____

_____

2. What methods could be used to prevent the male from hurting the female?

_____

_____

_____

_____

3. Based on this investigation, what other questions might you like to investigate?

_____

_____

_____

_____

Animal Behavior · *Laboratory Investigation*

More to Explore

New Problem Choose the response that interests you most from question 3 of Critical Thinking and Applications. Plan to investigate this problem.

Possible Materials Consider which materials you can use from this lab. What other materials might you need?

Safety Wash your hands after handling fish.

Procedure Make a hypothesis based on the question you want to investigate. Upon what information do you base your hypothesis? Write your procedure on a separate sheet of paper. Include a control with which to compare your results. Have the teacher approve your procedure before carrying out the investigation.

Observations Make a data table similar to the one for this lab.

Analyze and Conclude

1. Did your results support your hypothesis? Explain your answer.

   _____

   _____

   _____

2. Evaluate your procedure. What worked well? If you were to repeat this experiment, what parts of the procedure would you change?

   _____

   _____

   _____

   _____

Bones, Muscles, and Skin · *Skills Lab*

A Look Beneath the Skin

Problem

What are some characteristics of skeletal muscles? How do skeletal muscles work?

Skills Focus

observing, inferring, classifying

Materials

water
paper towels
scissors
dissecting tray
uncooked chicken wing, treated with bleach

Procedure

1. Put on goggles, an apron, and protective gloves. **CAUTION:** *Wear gloves whenever you handle the chicken.*

2. Your teacher will give you a chicken wing. Rinse it well with water, dry it with paper towels, and place it in a dissecting tray.

3. Carefully extend the wing to find out how many major parts it has. Draw a diagram of the external structure. Label the upper arm, elbow, lower arm, and hand (wing tip).

4. Use scissors to remove the skin. Cut only through the skin. **CAUTION:** *Cut away from your body and your classmates.*

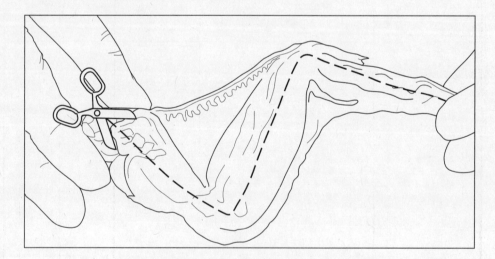

Bones, Muscles, and Skin • *Skills Lab*

5. Examine the muscles, the bundles of pink tissue around the bones. Find the two groups of muscles in the upper arm. Hold the arm down at the shoulder, and alternately pull on each muscle group. Observe what happens.

6. Find the two groups of muscles in the lower arm. Hold down the arm at the elbow, and alternately pull on each muscle group. Then make a diagram of the wing's muscles.

7. Find the tendons—shiny white tissue at the ends of the muscles. Notice what parts the tendons connect. Add the tendons to your diagram.

8. Remove the muscles and tendons. Find the ligaments, which are the whitish ribbon-shaped structures between bones. Add them to your diagram.

9. Dispose of the chicken parts according to your teacher's instructions. Wash your hands.

Analyze and Conclude

Write your answers on a separate sheet of paper.

1. **Observing** How does a chicken wing move at the elbow? How does the motion compare to how your elbow moves? What type of joint is involved?

2. **Inferring** What happened when you pulled on one of the arm muscles? What muscle action does the pulling represent?

3. **Classifying** Categorize the muscles you observed as smooth, cardiac, or skeletal.

4. **Communicating** Why is it valuable to record your observations with accurate diagrams? Write a paragraph in which you describe what your diagrams show.

More to Explore

Use the procedures from this lab to examine an uncooked chicken thigh and leg. Compare how the chicken leg and a human leg move. *Obtain your teacher's permission before carrying out your investigation.*

Bones, Muscles, and Skin · *Design Your Own Lab*

Sun Safety

Problem

How well do different materials protect the skin from the sun?

Skills Focus

observing, predicting, interpreting data, drawing conclusions

Materials

scissors

photosensitive paper

metric ruler

white construction paper

stapler

pencil

resealable plastic bag

plastic knife

2 sunscreens with SPF ratings of 4 and 30

staple remover

3 different fabrics

Procedure

PART 1 Sunscreen Protection

1. Read over the procedure for Part 1. Then, write a prediction about how well each of the sunscreens will protect against the sun.

2. Use scissors to cut two strips of photosensitive paper that measure 5 cm by 15 cm.

3. Divide each strip into thirds by drawing lines across the strips.

4. Cover one third of each strip with a square of white construction paper. Staple each square down.

Bones, Muscles, and Skin ▪ *Design Your Own Lab*

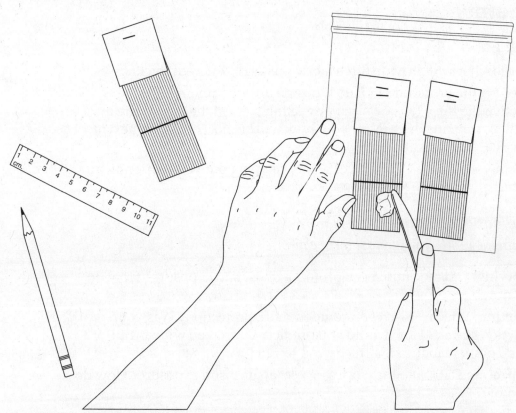

5. Use a pencil to write the lower SPF rating on the back of the first strip. Write the other SPF rating on the back of the second strip.

6. Place the two strips side by side in a plastic bag. Seal the bag, then staple through the white squares to hold the strips in place.

7. With a plastic knife, spread a thin layer of each sunscreen on the bag over the bottom square of its labeled strip. This is shown in the diagram above. Make certain each strip has the same thickness of sunscreen. Be sure not to spread sunscreen over the middle squares.

8. Place the strips in sunlight until the color of the middle squares stops changing. Make sure the bag is sunscreen-side up when you place it in the sunlight.

9. Remove the staples from the bag, and then take out the strips. Take off the construction paper. Rinse the strips for one minute in cold water, then dry them flat.

10. Observe all the squares. Then, record your observations.

Bones, Muscles, and Skin · *Design Your Own Lab*

Sun Safety *(continued)*

PART 2 Fabric Protection

11. Your teacher will provide three fabric pieces of different thicknesses.

12. Based on the procedure in Part 1, design an experiment to test how effective the three fabrics are in protecting against the sun. Write a prediction about which fabric you think will be most effective, next most effective, and least effective.

13. Obtain your teacher's approval before carrying out your experiment. Record all of your observations.

Analyze and Conclude

Write your answers on a separate sheet of paper.

1. **Observing** Did the sunscreens protect against sun exposure? How do you know?

2. **Predicting** Which sunscreen provided more protection? Was your prediction correct? How would you predict a sunscreen with an SPF of 15 would compare to the sunscreens you tested?

3. **Interpreting Data** Did the fabrics protect against sun exposure? How do you know?

4. **Drawing Conclusions** Which of the fabrics provided the most protection? The least protection? How did your results compare with your predictions?

5. **Communicating** What advice would you give people about protecting their skin from the sun? Create a pamphlet in which you address this question by comparing the different sunscreens and fabrics you tested.

More to Explore

Design another experiment, this time to find out whether ordinary window glass protects skin against sun exposure. *Obtain your teacher's permission before carrying out your investigation.*

Bones, Muscles, and Skin • *Laboratory Investigation*

Examining Bones, Muscles, and Skin

Pre-Lab Discussion

Have you ever seen a picture of a jellyfish? The body of the animal has no rigid shape because it has no bones. Think of what your body would be like without bones. Bones provide the structure needed for you to stand upright and to hold this paper. Bones work closely with muscles to allow your body to move. Muscles also keep important parts of your body, such as your heart, working. In Part A of the following investigation, you will examine bone and muscle cells to see how their structure relates to what they do.

Of course, you can't see your bones and muscles. They are covered by the largest organ in your body—your skin. What does skin do? One of its many purposes is to protect the inside of your body against injury and disease. It also contains sense receptors that give you your sense of touch. In Part B of this investigation, you will examine one important function of the sense of touch—the ability to distinguish different temperatures.

1. What are the three types of muscles? Explain how they differ.

   _____

   _____

   _____

2. Name three functions of bones and three functions of skin.

   _____

   _____

   _____

Problem

How are the three types of muscle cells and bone cells alike, and how do they differ? How does your body sense differences in temperature?

Materials *(per group)*
prepared slides of
    smooth muscle
    skeletal muscle
    cardiac muscle
    cross-section of compact human bone
microscope
3 transparent plastic cups
cold water
room-temperature water
paper towel
clock or watch with a second hand

Bones, Muscles, and Skin ▪ *Laboratory Investigation*

Examining Bones, Muscles, and Skin (continued)

Safety 🔲 *Review the safety guidelines in Appendix A of your textbook.*
Use caution when handling the microscope slides. If they break, tell the teacher. Do not pick up broken glass.

Procedure

Part A: Observing Bone and Muscle

1. Using the microscope, first on low power and then on high power, examine a prepared slide of skeletal muscle. Look for nuclei in the cells.

2. In Part A of Observations, sketch the skeletal muscle tissue that you see. Note the magnification you use to view it. Label details of the cells such as striations (stripes) and nuclei.

3. Using the microscope, first on low power and then on high power, examine a prepared slide of cardiac muscle. Look for nuclei in the cells.

4. In Observations, sketch the cardiac muscle tissue that you see. Note the magnification you use to view it. Label details of the cells.

5. Using the microscope, first on low power and then on high power, examine a prepared slide of smooth muscle. Look for nuclei in the cells.

6. In Observations, sketch the smooth muscle tissue that you see. Note the magnification you use to view it. Label details of the cells.

7. Using the microscope, first on low power and then on high power, examine a prepared slide of compact bone. Look for cells and structural features.

8. In Observations, sketch the bone tissue that you see. Note the magnification you use to view it. Label details of the structures.

Part B: Examining the Sense of Touch

1. Place a cup of cold water and a cup of room-temperature water on two or three paper towels in front of you. Put your index finger in the cold water for about 5 seconds.

2. Remove your finger from the cold water, and put it in the room-temperature water. Immediately tell your partner how the water feels. For this step and each of the following steps, have your partner record all your observations in the Data Table.

3. Leave your finger in the room-temperature water. Describe how the water feels after a few minutes.

4. While one finger is still in the water, put your index finger from your other hand in the same cup.

5. Remove both fingers from the water. Put your original finger into the cold water and leave it there for about 20 seconds. Then move it into the room-temperature water. Leave your finger in the cup for a few minutes.

6. Put your other index finger into the room-temperature water. Compare how the water feels now to how it felt in Step 3.

7. Remove both fingers from the water.

Bones, Muscles, and Skin ▪ *Laboratory Investigation*

Observations

Part A

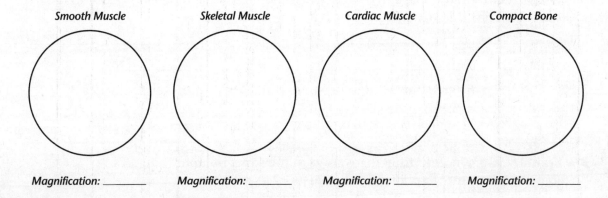

Smooth Muscle   Skeletal Muscle   Cardiac Muscle   Compact Bone

Magnification: _____   Magnification: _____   Magnification: _____   Magnification: _____

Part B

Step	What to Observe	Observations
2	How did the water feel when you first put your finger in the room-temperature water?	
3	How did the water feel when you left your finger in the room-temperature water?	
4	How did the water feel to your other finger when you put it in the room-temperature water?	
5	How did the water feel when you first put your finger in the room-temperature water this second time?	
6	How did the water feel when you left your finger in the room-temperature water this second time?	
7	How does the water feel now compared to how it felt in Step 5?	

Bones, Muscles, and Skin • *Laboratory Investigation*

Examining Bones, Muscles, and Skin (continued)

Analyze and Conclude

1. What structure can you clearly see in the muscle cells that you cannot see in the bone? Describe this structure.

   _____

   _____

2. What is the main structural difference between cardiac and skeletal muscle?

   _____

   _____

3. Did the sensors in your fingers respond in the same manner to the room-temperature water? Explain your answer.

   _____

   _____

   _____

Critical Thinking and Applications

1. Can you infer that striations, or stripes, have anything to do with whether a muscle is voluntary or involuntary? Explain.

   _____

   _____

2. You looked at a cross-section of a bone. Describe how you could model the interior structure of an entire bone.

   _____

   _____

3. Suppose one person has been outdoors on a hot day and another person has been in an air-conditioned room. They both go into an area that is at room temperature. Use your results from Part B to explain the temperature sensed by both people in the room of new location.

   _____

   _____

   _____

More to Explore

Repeat Part B of this experiment, using warm water in place of cold water.
CAUTION: *Do not use water that is hot enough to burn you or cause discomfort.*
Record all of your observations in a table similar to the one used in Part B.

Food and Digestion ▪ *Consumer Lab*

Raisin' the Raisin Question

Problem

Raisins are a good source of the mineral iron. Which raisin bran cereal contains the most raisins?

Skills Focus

measuring, calculating, controlling variables

Materials

balance

paper towels

beaker (250 mL)

raisin bran cereals (several brands)

Procedure

1. Use a balance to find the mass of a clean 250-mL beaker. Record the mass in the data table below.

2. Fill the beaker to the top with one of the brands of raisin bran cereal, but do not pack down the cereal. **CAUTION:** *Do not put any cereal in your mouth.* Write the brand name in the data table. Measure and record the mass of the beaker plus cereal. Subtract the mass of the empty beaker to get the mass of the cereal alone. Record the result.

3. Pour the cereal onto a paper towel. Separate the raisins from the bran and place the raisins back in the beaker. Measure and record the mass of the beaker plus raisins. Subtract the mass of the empty beaker to get the mass of the raisins alone. Record the result.

4. Repeat Steps 1–3 with each of the other brands of cereal.

	Data Table					
	Mass (g)					**Percentage Mass of Raisins(%)**
Cereal Brand	**Empty Beaker**	**Beaker plus Cereal**	**Cereal**	**Beaker plus Raisins**	**Raisins**	

Food and Digestion · *Consumer Lab*

Raisin' the Raisin Question *(continued)*

Analyze and Conclude

1. **Measuring** Why did you first measure the mass of an empty beaker and then the mass of the beaker plus cereal?

   _____

   _____

   _____

2. **Calculating** Calculate the percentage mass of raisins in each cereal as follows:

   $$\% \text{ Mass of raisins } = \frac{\text{Mass of raisins}}{\text{Mass of cereal}} \times 100\%$$

   Record the result in your data table.

3. **Interpreting Data** Based on your observations, which brand of cereal had the greatest percentage of raisins by mass?

   _____

   _____

   _____

4. **Controlling Variables** Was it important that all of the cereal samples were collected in the same-size beaker? Explain.

   _____

   _____

   _____

5. **Communicating** Based on your results, write a paragraph that could be printed on a box of raisin bran cereal that would help consumers understand that this brand is the best source of iron.

   _____

   _____

   _____

Design an Experiment

In this investigation, you examined a *sample* of cereal rather than the contents of the entire box. Scientists often use samples because it is a more practical way to make observations. Redesign this experiment to improve upon the sampling technique and increase the accuracy of your results. *Obtain your teacher's permission before carrying out your investigation.*

Food and Digestion · *Skills Lab*

As the Stomach Churns

Problem

What conditions are needed for the digestion of proteins in the stomach?

Skills Focus

interpreting data, controlling variables, drawing conclusions

Materials

test-tube rack

pepsin

water

4 strips of blue litmus paper

cubes of boiled egg white

10-mL plastic graduated cylinder

4 test tubes with stoppers

marking pencil

dilute hydrochloric acid

plastic stirrers

Procedure

1. In this lab, you will investigate how acidic conditions affect protein digestion. Read over the entire lab to see what materials you will be testing. Write a prediction stating which conditions you think will speed up protein digestion.

2. Label four test tubes *A, B, C,* and *D* and place them in a test-tube rack.

3. In this lab, the protein you will test is boiled egg white, which has been cut into cubes about 1 cm on each side. Add 3 cubes to each test tube. Note and record the size and overall appearance of the cubes in each test tube. **CAUTION:** *Do not put any egg white into your mouth.*

4. Use a graduated cylinder to add 10 mL of the enzyme pepsin to test tube A. Observe the egg white cubes to determine whether an immediate reaction takes place. Record your observations under Day 1 in your data table. If no changes occur, write "no immediate reaction."

5. Use a clean graduated cylinder to add 5 mL of pepsin to test tube B. Then rinse the graduated cylinder and add 5 mL of water to test tube B. Observe whether or not an immediate reaction takes place.

Food and Digestion • *Skills Lab*

As the Stomach Churns (continued)

6. Use a clean graduated cylinder to add 10 mL of hydrochloric acid to test tube C. Observe whether or not an immediate reaction takes place. **CAUTION:** *Hydrochloric acid can burn skin and clothing. Avoid direct contact with it. Wash any splashes or spills with plenty of water, and notify your teacher.*

7. Use a clean graduated cylinder to add 5 mL of pepsin to test tube D. Then rinse the graduated cylinder and add 5 mL of hydrochloric acid to test tube D. Observe whether or not an immediate reaction takes place. Record your observations.

8. Obtain four strips of blue litmus paper. (Blue litmus paper turns pink in the presence of an acid.) Dip a clean plastic stirrer into the solution in each test tube, and then touch the stirrer to a piece of litmus paper. Observe what happens to the litmus paper. Record your observations.

9. Insert stoppers in the four test tubes and store the test tube rack as directed by your teacher.

10. The next day, examine the contents of each test tube. Note any changes in the size and overall appearance of the egg white cubes. Then test each solution with litmus paper. Record your observations in your data table.

	Data Table			
Test Tube	**Egg White Appearance**		**Litmus Color**	
	Day 1	**Day 2**	**Day 1**	**Day 2**
A				
B				
C				
D				

Food and Digestion · *Skills Lab*

Analyze and Conclude

Write your answers on a separate sheet of paper.

1. **Interpreting Data** Which materials were the best at digesting the egg white? What observations enabled you to determine this?
2. **Inferring** Is the chemical digestion of protein in food a fast reaction or a slow reaction? Explain.
3. **Controlling Variables** Why was it important that the cubes of egg white all be about the same size?
4. **Drawing Conclusions** What did this lab show about the ability of pepsin to digest protein?
5. **Communicating** Write a paragraph in which you describe the purpose of test tube A and test tube C as they relate to the steps you followed in the procedure.

Design an Experiment

Design a way to test whether protein digestion is affected by the size of the food pieces. Write down your hypothesis and the procedure you will follow. *Obtain your teacher's permission before carrying out your investigation.*

Food and Digestion • *Laboratory Investigation*

Nutrient Identification

Pre-Lab Discussion

Do you know what foods have a lot of protein? Plenty of carbohydrates? Carbohydrates, fats, proteins, vitamins, minerals, and water are all nutrients in your food. You can detect the presence of some of these nutrients by taste. For example, all foods that taste sweet contain some form of sugar unless they are artificially sweetened. On the other hand, some foods, such as milk and onions, contain sugar but do not taste sweet. Therefore, scientists do not rely on taste or appearance to determine what nutrients a food contains. They use other tests to identify nutrients.

In this investigation, you will perform tests to detect starches, sugars, and proteins in foods.

1. What are the two groups of carbohydrates? What are their common names?

   _____

   _____

2. What functions do proteins perform in your body?

   _____

   _____

Problem

How can you determine what nutrients are in various kinds of food?

Materials *(per group)*

samples of various foods, including flour, honey, and gelatin

paper towels

3 medicine droppers

iodine solution

hot plate

beaker, 400 mL

water

2 test tubes

Benedict's solution

test-tube holder

Biuret solution

Food and Digestion · *Laboratory Investigation*

Safety

       Review the safety guidelines in Appendix A of your textbook.

Iodine solution and Biuret solution can stain skin and clothing. Benedict's solution can burn skin. If you spill any of these solutions on your skin, rinse it off immediately with cold running water and tell the teacher. Use a test-tube holder and heat-resistant gloves when handling hot test tubes.

Procedure

Part A: Test for Starches

1. Place a small amount of flour on a paper towel.

2. Use a medicine dropper to put 1 or 2 drops of iodine solution on the flour.
   CAUTION: *Keep iodine solution off your skin because it will leave a stain.*

3. Notice that the iodine solution turns purplish blue or blue-black. This color change indicates that flour contains starch. If the iodine remains yellow-brown, starch is not present.

4. Choose two to five other foods to test. Predict whether each food contains starch. Give a reason for your prediction.

   _____

   _____

   _____

5. Test these additional foods for the presence of starch and record your results in Data Table 1.

Part B: Test for Sugars

1. Set up a hot-water bath by placing a beaker half full of water on a hot plate and starting to heat the water.

2. Use a medicine dropper to put 30 drops of honey-and-water solution in a test tube.

3. Use another medicine dropper to add Benedict's solution until the test tube is about one-third full. **CAUTION:** *Keep Benedict's solution away from your skin because it can burn you. If you spill some on you, rinse it off immediately with cold running water and inform the teacher.*

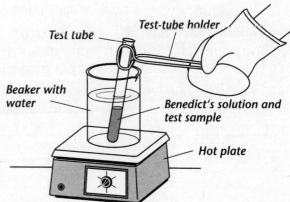

Test-tube holder

Test tube

Beaker with water

Benedict's solution and test sample

Hot plate

Food and Digestion ▪ *Laboratory Investigation*

Nutrient Identification (continued)

4. Wait until the water in the water bath is boiling. **CAUTION:** *Be careful when using the water bath. Adjust the heat so that the water does not boil too vigorously. Take care not to point the opening of the test tube toward anyone. Remember to wear your safety goggles.* Use a test-tube holder to hold the test tube upright in the water bath. See Figure 1. Gently boil the mixture for 2 to 5 minutes.

5. Remove the test tube from the water bath. The solution should have turned green, yellow, orange, or orange-red. Any of these colors indicates that sugar is present. If the Benedict's solution remains blue, sugar is not present. Note: Benedict's solution indicates the presence of simple sugars such as glucose and fructose, which are found in most fruits. It does not detect the presence of complex sugars such as lactose (milk sugar).

6. Choose two to five additional foods to test. If you use solid foods, crush the material to be tested, put it in a test tube, and add 30 drops of water. If you use liquids, test 30 drops.

7. Predict whether each of these foods contains sugar. Give a reason for your prediction.

_____

_____

_____

8. Test these additional foods for sugar and record your results in Data Table 2.

Test C: Test for Proteins

1. Use a medicine dropper to fill a test tube about one-third full of gelatin solution.

2. Add 10 drops of Biuret solution. **CAUTION:** *Biuret solution will burn skin and clothing. If you spill any solution on yourself, rinse it off immediately with cold running water and inform your teacher.*

3. Hold the tube against a white background. Notice that the mixture has turned violet. This color change indicates the presence of protein. If there is no color change, protein is not present.

4. Choose two to five other foods to test. Predict whether each contains protein. Give a reason for your prediction.

_____

_____

_____

5. Test these additional foods for protein and record your results in Data Table 3.

Food and Digestion ▪ *Laboratory Investigation*

Observations

Data Table 1

Food Tested	Color with Iodine Solution	Is Starch Present?
Flour	Purplish-black or blue-black	Yes

Data Table 2

Food Tested	Color with Benedict's Solution	Is Simple Sugar Present?
Honey and water	Green, yellow, orange, or orange-red	Yes

Data Table 3

Food Tested	Color with Biuret Solution	Is Protein Present?
Gelatin solution	Violet	Yes

Food and Digestion ▪ *Laboratory Investigation*

Nutrient Identification *(continued)*

Analyze and Conclude

1. Of the foods you tested, which contain starch? How do you know? Were your predictions correct?

_____

_____

_____

2. Of the foods you tested, which contain sugar? How do you know? Were your predictions correct?

_____

_____

_____

3. Of the foods you tested, which contain protein? How do you know? Were your predictions correct?

_____

_____

_____

Critical Thinking and Applications

1. If a food does not turn Biuret solution violet, do you know what nutrients the food contains? Give a reason for your answer.

_____

_____

_____

2. Why is it important to include starches, sugars, and proteins in your diet?

_____

_____

3. Write at least two new questions about other nutrients (such as minerals, vitamins, and so forth) that might be in the foods you tested.

_____

_____

_____

_____

Food and Digestion ▪ *Laboratory Investigation*

4. Briefly, how would you go about answering your questions above?

_____

_____

_____

_____

_____

More to Explore

Chemical tests can detect different vitamins in foods. Indophenol is a chemical that tests for vitamin C. To conduct this test, wear safety goggles and a lab apron. Pour indophenol into a test tube to a depth of 2 cm. Add the substance to be tested, one drop at a time. Keep track of the number of drops added and shake the test tube after each drop is added. Continue until the blue color disappears. The more drops of test substance required to eliminate the blue color, the less vitamin C the substance contains. Compare the vitamin C content of various fruit juices, such as orange, apple, grapefruit, or lemon, or various brands of one kind of juice. (**CAUTION:** *Do not perform any experiment unless the teacher approves your written plan.*)

Circulation · *Skills Lab*

Heart Beat, Health Beat
Problem
How does physical activity affect your pulse rate?

Skills Focus
graphing, interpreting data, drawing conclusions

Materials
graph paper

watch with second hand or heart rate monitor

Procedure

1. Predict how your pulse rate will change as you go from resting to being active, then back to resting again.

2. Locate your pulse by placing the index and middle finger of one hand on your other wrist at the base of your thumb. Move the two fingers slightly until you feel your pulse. If you are using a heart rate monitor, see your teacher for instructions.

3. Work with a partner for the rest of this lab. Begin by determining your resting pulse rate. Count the number of beats in your pulse for exactly 1 minute while your partner times you. Record your resting heart rate in your data table. **CAUTION:** *Do not complete the rest of these procedures if there is any medical reason why you should avoid physical activities.*

4. Walk in place for 1 minute while your partner times you. Stop and immediately take your pulse for 1 minute. Record the number in your data table.

5. Run in place for 1 minute. Take your pulse again, and record the result.

6. Sit down right away, and have your partner time you as you rest for 1 minute. Then take your pulse rate again.

7. Have your partner time you as you rest for 3 more minutes. Then take your pulse rate again and record it.

Circulation ▪ *Skills Lab*

Data Table

Activity	Pulse Rate
Resting	
Walking	
Running	
Resting after exercise (1 min)	
Resting after exercise (3+ min)	

Analyze and Conclude

Write your answers on a separate sheet of paper.

1. **Graphing** Use the data you obtained to create a bar graph of your pulse rate under the different conditions you tested.

2. **Interpreting Data** What happens to the pulse rate when the physical activity has stopped?

3. **Inferring** What can you infer about the heartbeat when the pulse rate increases?

4. **Drawing Conclusions** What conclusion can you draw about the relationship between physical activity and a person's pulse rate?

5. **Communicating** How could you improve the accuracy of your pulse measurements? Write a paragraph in which you discuss this question in relation to the steps you followed in your procedure.

Design an Experiment

Design an experiment to determine whether the resting pulse rates of adults, teens, and young children differ. *Obtain your teacher's permission before carrying out your investigation.*

Circulation • *Skills Lab*

Do You Know Your A-B-O's?

Problem

Which blood types can safely receive transfusions of type A blood? Which can receive type O blood?

Skills Focus

interpreting data, drawing conclusions

Materials

4 paper cups

8 plastic petri dishes

marking pen

4 plastic droppers

white paper

toothpicks

four model "blood" types

Procedure

1. Write down your ideas about why type O blood might be in higher demand than other blood types.

2. Label four paper cups A, B, AB, and O. Fill each cup about one-third full with the model "blood" supplied by your teacher. Insert one clean plastic dropper into each cup. Use each dropper to transfer only that one type of blood.

3. Label the side of each of four petri dishes with a blood type: A, B, AB, or O. Place the petri dishes on a sheet of white paper.

4. Use the plastic droppers to place 10 drops of each type of blood in its labeled petri dish. Each sample represents the blood of a potential receiver of a blood transfusion. Record the original color of each sample in your data table as yellow, blue, green, or colorless.

5. Label your first data table Donor: Type A. To test whether each potential receiver can safely receive type A blood, add 10 drops of type A blood to each sample. Stir each mixture with a separate, clean toothpick.

6. Record the final color of each mixture in the data table. If the color stayed the same, write "safe" in the last column. If the color of the mixture changed, write "unsafe."

7. Label your second data table Donor: Type O. Obtain four clean petri dishes, and repeat Steps 3 through 6 to determine who could safely receive type O blood.

Circulation ▪ *Skills Lab*

Data Table

Donor: Type _____			
Potential Receiver	**Original Color**	**Final Color of Mixture**	**Safe or Unsafe?**
A			
B			
AB			
O			

Donor: Type _____			
Potential Receiver	**Original Color**	**Final Color of Mixture**	**Safe or Unsafe?**
A			
B			
AB			
O			

Analyze and Conclude

Write your answers on a separate sheet of paper.

1. **Interpreting Data** Which blood types can safely receive a transfusion of type A blood? Type O blood?
2. **Inferring** Use what you know about marker molecules to explain why some transfusions of type A blood are safe while others are unsafe.
3. **Drawing Conclusions** If some blood types are not available, how might type O blood be useful?
4. **Communicating** Write a paragraph in which you discuss why it is important for hospitals to have an adequate supply of different types of blood.

More to Explore

Repeat this activity to find out which blood types can safely receive donations of type B and type AB blood.

Circulation · *Laboratory Investigation*

Direction of Blood Flow

Pre-Lab Discussion

If you're healthy, you probably don't think much about your circulatory system. It just pumps along, keeping you alive. But think about this: liquids flow downhill. How can blood travel up to your heart, against the flow of gravity, as well as down? Somehow the muscle that is your heart and the arteries, veins, and capillaries work together to keep blood flowing to every part of your body.

In this investigation, you will demonstrate a feature of your veins that helps keep blood flowing throughout your body.

1. Compare and contrast the structures of arteries and veins.

   _____

   _____

   _____

2. Why is it essential that blood flow upward in the body?

   _____

   _____

   _____

Problem

What prevents blood from flowing backward toward the lower part of the body?

Materials

Safety ⚠ *Review the safety guidelines in Appendix A of your textbook.*

Be gentle when exerting pressure on veins.

Procedure

1. Work with two partners. Decide which partner will observe, which one will be the subject, and which one will record observations.

2. Have the subject stand with both arms down at his or her sides until the veins on the back of the hands stand out.

3. The subject should keep both arms down. The observer should put one finger from each hand next to each other on one of the subject's raised veins. See Figure 1.

4. The observer leaves the finger closest to the ground where it is. He or she slides the other finger upward along the vein for about 4 cm, pressing firmly but gently.

Circulation · *Laboratory Investigation*

5. The observer tells the recorder what happens to the vein. The recorder writes the observations in the Data Table.

6. The observer keeps the finger closest to the ground in place, then releases the upper finger. The observer tells the recorder what happens to the vein, and the recorder writes the observations in the Data Table.

7. The observer releases the finger that is still in place and tells the recorder what happens to the vein. The recorder writes the observations in the Data Table.

8. Everyone switches roles and repeats steps 2–7.

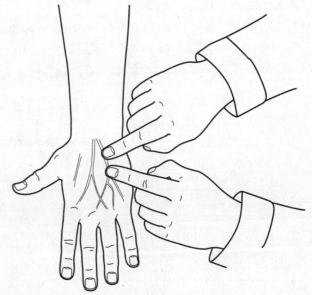

Figure 1

Observations

Data Table

Step	Effect on Vein	
	Subject 1	**Subject 2**
Observer moves fingers apart.		
Observer releases upper finger.		
Observer releases both fingers.		

Circulation • *Laboratory Investigation*

Direction of Blood Flow *(continued)*

Analyze and Conclude

1. How do veins and valves contribute to the effect you saw when the observer's fingers moved apart?

   _____

   _____

   _____

2. How do veins and valves contribute to the effect you saw when the observer released the upper finger?

   _____

   _____

3. How do veins and valves contribute to the effect you saw when the observer released both fingers?

   _____

   _____

4. Use your observations to summarize why blood doesn't flow backward in your body.

   _____

   _____

   _____

Critical Thinking and Applications

1. What would have happened if you had used an artery instead of a vein in this experiment?

   _____

   _____

   _____

2. In terms of circulation, why is it important to wear clothes that are not too tight? Include evidence from the lab in your answer.

   _____

   _____

   _____

3. Many buildings have plumbing in rooms that are below ground level, so the plumbing is lower than the building's drain pipe. Use what you learned in the investigation to explain how someone could design a bathtub drain in such a room. The drain water must not flow back into the bathtub.

   _____

   _____

Circulation • *Laboratory Investigation*

More to Explore

New Problem

When you exercise for cardiorespiratory fitness, you want your heart to beat at a target heart rate. What kind of exercise takes you closer to your target heart rate in 1 minute?

Possible Materials

Use a stopwatch or other timer with a second hand.

Safety

Do not exercise if you have health conditions, such as asthma, that might make exercise harmful.

Procedure

1. Take your pulse while resting, and calculate the low end of the range of your target heart rate. (Your target heart rate is the approximate heart rate you need to maintain during a workout in order to increase your endurance.) Use this formula to calculate the lower limit of your target heart rate:

$$\text{Target Heart Rate (in beats per minute)} = \left(210 - \text{resting pulse rate}\right)\left(0.6 + \text{resting pulse rate}\right)$$

2. Develop a procedure to determine whether 1 minute of jumping rope or 1 minute of running in place gets you closer to your target heart rate. On a separate sheet of paper, list the steps of your procedure. Have the teacher approve your procedure before you carry out the investigation.

Observations

Create a data table to record the resting heart rate, calculated target heart rate, and actual heart rate for both types of exercise.

Analyze and Conclude

1. Why do different exercises affect how long it takes you to reach your target heart rate?

   _____

   _____

2. Why do you think it is important for the heart rate to stay in the target range?

   _____

   _____

Respiration and Excretion · *Skills Lab*

A Breath of Fresh Air

Problem

What causes your body to inhale and exhale air?

Skills Focus

making models, observing, drawing conclusions

Materials

small balloon

large balloon

scissors

transparent plastic bottle with narrow neck

Procedure

1. In your notebook, explain how you think air gets into the lungs during the breathing process.

2. Cut off and discard the bottom of a small plastic bottle. Trim the cut edge so there are no rough spots.

3. Stretch a small balloon, then blow it up a few times to stretch it further. Insert the round end of the balloon through the mouth of the bottle. Then, with a partner holding the bottle, stretch the neck of the balloon and pull it over the mouth of the bottle.

4. Stretch a large balloon; then blow it up a few times to stretch it further. Cut off the balloon's neck, and discard the neck.

5. Have a partner hold the bottle while you stretch the remaining part of the balloon over the bottom opening of the bottle, as shown in the diagram.

6. Use one hand to hold the bottle firmly. With the knuckles of your other hand, push upward on the large balloon, causing it to form a dome. Remove your knuckles from the balloon, letting it flatten. Repeat this procedure a few times. Observe what happens to the small balloon. Record your observations in your notebook.

Respiration and Excretion ▪ *Skills Lab*

Analyze and Conclude

Write your answers on a separate sheet of paper.

1. **Making Models** Make a diagram of the completed model in your notebook. Add labels to show which parts of your model represent the chest cavity, diaphragm, lungs, and trachea.

2. **Observing** In this model, what is the position of the "diaphragm" just after you have made the model "exhale"? What do the lungs look like just after you have exhaled?

3. **Drawing Conclusions** In this model, how does the "diaphragm" move? How do these movements of the "diaphragm" affect the "lungs"?

4. **Communicating** Write a paragraph describing how this model shows that pressure changes are responsible for breathing.

More to Explore

How could you improve on this model to show more closely what happens in the chest cavity during the process of breathing? *Obtain your teacher's permission before carrying out your investigation.*

Respiration and Excretion · *Skills Lab*

Clues About Health

Problem

How can you test urine for the presence of glucose and protein?

Skills Focus

observing, interpreting data, drawing conclusions

Materials

6 test tubes

test-tube rack

6 plastic droppers

water

glucose solution

protein solution

marking pencil

white paper towels

6 glucose test strips

Biuret solution

3 simulated urine samples

Procedure

PART 1: Testing for Glucose

1. Label six test tubes as follows: *W* for water, *G* for glucose, *P* for protein, and *A*, *B*, and *C* for three patients' "urine samples." Place the test tubes in a test-tube rack.

2. Label six glucose test strips with the same letters: *W*, *G*, *P*, *A*, *B*, and *C*.

3. Note that on the page after the next page, there is a data table in which you can record your observations.

4. Fill each test tube about $\frac{3}{4}$ full with the solution that corresponds to its label.

5. Place glucose test strip W on a clean, dry section on a paper towel. Then use a clean plastic dropper to place 2 drops of the water from test tube W on the test strip. Record the resulting color of the test strip in your data table. If no color change occurs, write "no reaction."

6. Use the procedure in Step 5 to test each of the other five solutions with the correctly labeled glucose test strip. Record the color of each test strip in the data table.

Respiration and Excretion ▪ *Skills Lab*

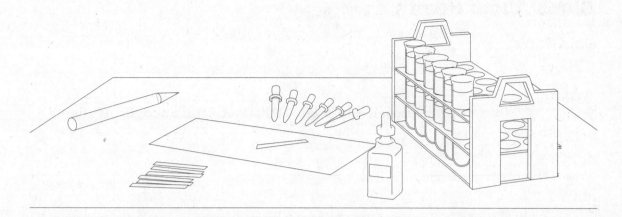

PART 2: Testing for Protein

7. Obtain a dropper bottle containing Biuret solution. Record the original color of the solution in your notebook.

8. Carefully add 30 drops of Biuret solution to test tube W. **CAUTION:** *Biuret solution can harm skin and damage clothing. Handle it with care.* Gently swirl the test tube to mix the two solutions together. Hold the test tube against a white paper towel to help you detect any color change. Observe the color of the final mixture, and record that color in your data table.

9. Repeat Step 8 for each of the other test tubes.

Respiration and Excretion · *Skills Lab*

Clues About Health *(continued)*

Data Table

Test for	W (water)	G (glucose)	P (protein)	A (Patient A)	B (Patient B)	C (Patient C)
Glucose						
Protein						

Analyze and Conclude

Write your answers on a separate sheet of paper.

Observing What color reaction occurred when you used the glucose test strip on sample W? On sample G?

Interpreting Data What do the changes in color you observed in Part I indicate? Explain.

Observing What happened when you added Biuret solution to test tube W? To test tube P?

Interpreting Data What do the changes in color of the Biuret solution you observed in Part II indicate? Explain.

Drawing Conclusions Which of the three patients' urine samples tested normal? How do you know?

Drawing Conclusions Which urine sample(s) indicated that diabetes might be present? How do you know?

Drawing Conclusions Which urine sample(s) indicated that kidney disease might be present? How do you know?

Communicating Do you think a doctor should draw conclusions about the presence of a disease based on a single urine sample? Write a paragraph in which you discuss this question based on what you know about gathering data in experiments.

More to Explore

Propose a way to determine whether a patient with glucose in the urine could reduce the level through changes in diet.

Respiration and Excretion · *Laboratory Investigation*

Measuring the Volume of Exhaled Air

Pre-Lab Discussion

If you have healthy lungs, you usually are not conscious of breathing. But have you ever felt like you were "out of breath"? Maybe you had to run to answer the phone or catch the school bus. Maybe you were ill, and your lungs were congested. Whatever the reason, you felt that the volume of air your lungs could hold was not enough for the amount of air you needed.

   The amount of air that lungs can hold varies from person to person. It also varies in any one person from time to time. In this investigation, you will design and use a plan to measure and compare the volume of air you exhale when you exercise and the volume of air you exhale when you are not exercising.

1. How does the respiratory system work?

   _____

   _____

   _____

2. Explain the difference between *breathing* and *respiration*.

   _____

   _____

Problem

How can you measure the volume of exhaled air?

Possible Materials *(per group)*

2-hole rubber stopper

2-L plastic bottle

glass tubing, long and short

rubber or flexible plastic tubing, 2 pieces

100-mL graduated cylinder

paper towels

cloth towel

glycerin

timer

Respiration and Excretion · *Laboratory Investigation*

Measuring the Volume of Exhaled Air *(continued)*

Safety

  Review the safety guidelines in Appendix A of your textbook.
When you blow through the tubing, first place a paper towel over the end of it and blow through the towel. Do not put your mouth directly on any of the tubing. If you insert glass tubing into the rubber stopper, use extreme caution and follow the teacher's instructions. Inform the teacher of any physical reasons you should not exercise. Your teacher must approve your plan before you can perform the experiment.

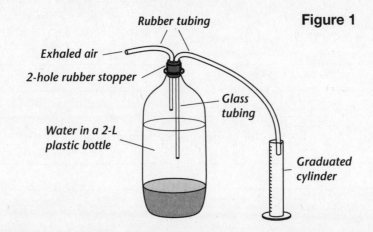

Figure 1

Rubber tubing

Exhaled air

2-hole rubber stopper

Glass tubing

Water in a 2-L plastic bottle

Graduated cylinder

Procedure

1. Read through this entire lab before you perform any part of it.

2. Use the materials listed here or other materials to assemble a spirometer—an instrument that can be used to measure the volume of air that your lungs can exhale. A spirometer is shown in Figure 1.

3. Plan how you will use your instrument to measure your lung volume. Consider what unit you will use for this measurement. On another sheet of paper, write a step-by-step plan for using your spirometer to measure the volume of your exhaled air.

4. Use Data Table 1 in Observations to record your data. You will need to record data for at least three trials; you may want to do more. You will then calculate the average volume of water displaced for all of your trials.

5. After the teacher has approved your plan, carry out your investigation. Then answer questions 1 and 2 in Observations.

6. After you have completed Data Table 1, run in place for two minutes. **CAUTION:** *Do not perform this part of the activity if you have any medical condition that makes the activity unsafe.* Repeat your experiment, using Data Table 2. Perform the same number of trials as before and average the trials. Then answer question 3 in Observations.

7. Rest for a few minutes until your breathing returns to normal. Then repeat the experiment using Data Table 3.

Respiration and Excretion • *Laboratory Investigation*

Observations

1. How is the volume of water that is forced out of the bottle related to the volume of air you exhale?

   _____

2. In the spirometer in Figure 1, why is it important that one glass tube is above the surface of the water and one glass tube is beneath it?

   _____

   _____

   _____

   _____

3. How does your average volume of exhaled air when you have not been exercising compare to your average volume of exhaled air right after you exercise?

   _____

   _____

   _____

Data Table 1 (before exercising)		Data Table 2 (after exercising)		Data Table 3 (when breathing returns to normal)	
Trial	**Volume of Water (mL)**	**Trial**	**Volume of Water (mL)**	**Trial**	**Volume of Water (mL)**
1		*1*		*1*	
2		*2*		*2*	
3		*3*		*3*	
Average		*Average*		*Average*	

Respiration and Excretion • *Laboratory Investigation*

Measuring the Volume of Exhaled Air (continued)

Analyze and Conclude

1. Why is it important to perform several trials for each part of the investigation?

   _____

   _____

2. Choose one of your data tables. Were the volumes the same for each trial? What could you change about your plan to assure that your data are more consistent?

   _____

   _____

   _____

3. Infer why the volume of air you exhaled after exercise differed from the volume you exhaled before exercising.

   _____

   _____

   _____

Critical Thinking and Applications

1. What might cause differences in lung volume among students in the class?

   _____

   _____

   _____

2. Denver, Colorado, is located at a high altitude. Miami, Florida, is located at sea level. Predict how the average Data Table 1 results for students who live in Denver compare to those of students who live in Miami. Explain your reasoning.

   _____

   _____

   _____

More to Explore

How could you determine the total volume of air someone can exhale in one minute? Write a procedure that you would follow to answer this question. Have your teacher approve your procedure before you carry out the investigation.

Fighting Disease • *Skills Lab*

The Skin as a Barrier

Problem

How does skin act as a barrier to pathogens?

Skills Focus

observing, making models,
controlling variables

Materials

4 sealable plastic bags

4 fresh apples

rotting apple

cotton swabs

marking pen

paper towels

toothpick

rubbing alcohol

Procedure

Review the safety guidelines in Appendix A.

1. Read over the entire procedure to see how you will treat each of four fresh apples. Write a prediction in your notebook about the change(s) you expect to see in each apple.

2. Label four plastic bags *1, 2, 3,* and *4.*

3. Wash your hands with soap and water. Then, gently wash four fresh apples with water and dry them carefully with paper towels. Place one apple in plastic bag 1, and seal the bag.

4. Insert a toothpick tip into a rotting apple and withdraw it. Lightly draw the tip of the toothpick down the side of the second apple without breaking the skin. Repeat these actions three more times, touching the toothpick to different parts of the apple without breaking the skin. Insert the apple into plastic bag 2, and seal the bag.

5. Insert the toothpick tip into the rotting apple and withdraw it. Use the tip to make a long, thin scratch down the side of the third apple. Be sure to pierce the apple's skin. Repeat these actions three more times, making additional scratches on different parts of the apple. Insert the apple into plastic bag 3, and seal the bag.

Fighting Disease · *Skills Lab*

The Skin as a Barrier *(continued)*

6. Repeat Step 5 with the fourth apple. However, before you place the apple into the bag, dip a cotton swab in rubbing alcohol, and swab the scratches. Then place the apple into plastic bag 4, and seal the bag. **CAUTION:** *Alcohol and its vapors are flammable. Work where there are no sparks, exposed flames, or other heat sources.*

7. Store the four bags in a warm, dark place. Wash your hands thoroughly with soap and water.

8. Every day for one week, remove the apples from their storage place and observe them without opening the bags. Record your observations, and return the bags to their storage location. At the end of the activity, dispose of the unopened bags as directed by your teacher.

Data Table

Date	Apple 1 (no contact with decay)	Apple 2 (contact with decay, unbroken skin)	Apple 3 (contact with decay, scratched, untreated)	Apple 4 (contact with decay, scratched, treated with alcohol)

Analyze and Conclude

Write your answers on a separate sheet of paper.

1. **Observing** How did the appearance of the four apples compare?
2. **Interpreting Data** Explain the differences you observed in Question 1.
3. **Making Models** In this experiment, what condition in the human body is each of the four fresh apples supposed to model?
4. **Controlling Variables** What is the purpose of Apple 1 in this experiment? Explain.
5. **Making Models** What is the role of the rotting apple in this experiment?
6. **Communicating** Write a paragraph in which you explain how this investigation shows why routine cuts and scrapes should be cleaned and bandaged.

Design an Experiment

Using apples as you did in this activity, design an experiment to model how washing hands can prevent the spread of disease. *Obtain your teacher's permission before carrying out your investigation.*

Fighting Disease · *Skills Lab*

Causes of Death, Then and Now

Problem

How do the leading causes of death today compare with those in 1900?

Skills Focus

graphing, interpreting data, drawing conclusions

Materials

colored pencils

ruler

calculator (optional)

protractor

compass

Procedure

1. The data table on the next page shows the leading causes of death in the United States in 1900 and today. Examine the data and note that one cause of death—accidents—is not a disease. The other causes are labeled either "I," indicating an infectious disease, or "NI," indicating a noninfectious disease.

PART 1 Comparing Specific Causes of Death

2. Look at the following causes of death in the data table: (a) pneumonia and influenza, (b) heart disease, (c) accidents, and (d) cancer. Construct a bar graph that compares the numbers of deaths from each of those causes in 1900 and today. Label the horizontal axis *"Causes of Death."* Label the vertical axis *"Deaths per 100,000 People."* Draw two bars side by side for each cause of death. Use a key to show which bars refer to 1900 and which refer to today.

PART 2 Comparing Infectious and Noninfectious Causes of Death

3. In this part of the lab, you will make two circle graphs showing three categories: infectious diseases, noninfectious diseases, and "other." You may want to review the information on creating circle graphs in the Skills Handbook.

Fighting Disease ▪ *Skills Lab*

Causes of Death, Then and Now *(continued)*

Ten Leading Causes of Death in the United States, 1900 and Today			
1900		**Today**	
Cause of Death	**Deaths per 100,000**	**Cause of Death**	**Deaths per 100,000**
Pneumonia, influenza (I)*	215	Heart disease (NI)	246
Tuberculosis (I)	185	Cancer (NI)	194
Diarrhea (I)	140	Stroke (NI)	57
Heart disease (NI)	130	Lung disease (NI)	43
Stroke (NI)	110	Accidents	34
Kidney disease (NI)	85	Diabetes (NI)	25
Accidents	75	Pneumonia, influenza (I)	22
Cancer (NI)	65	Alzheimer's disease (NI)	19
Senility (NI)	55	Kidney disease (NI)	14
Diphtheria (I)	40	Septicemia (I)	11
Total	**1,100**	**Total**	**665**

* (I) indicates an infectious disease. (NI) indicates a noninfectious disease.

4. Start by grouping the data from 1900 into the three categories—infectious diseases, noninfectious diseases, and other causes. Calculate the total number of deaths for each category. Then find the size of the "pie slice" (the number of degrees) for each category, and construct your circle graph. To find the size of the infectious disease slice for 1900, for example, use the following formula:

$$\frac{\text{Number of deaths from infectious diseases}}{1{,}100 \text{ deaths total}} = \frac{x}{360°}$$

5. Calculate the percentage represented by each category using this formula:

$$\frac{\text{Numbers of degrees in a slice}}{360°} \times 100 = \blacksquare\%$$

6. Repeat Steps 4 and 5 using the data from today to make the second circle graph. What part of the formula in Step 4 do you need to change?

Fighting Disease ▪ *Skills Lab*

Analyze and Conclude

1. **Observing** What information did you learn from examining the data table in Step 1?

2. **Graphing** According to your bar graph, which cause of death showed the greatest increase between 1900 and today? The greatest decrease?

3. **Interpreting Data** In your circle graphs, which category decreased the most from 1900 to today? Which increased the most?

4. **Drawing Conclusions** Suggest an explanation for the change in the number of deaths due to infectious diseases from 1900 to today.

5. **Communicating** In a paragraph, explain how graphs help you identify patterns and other information in data that you might otherwise overlook.

More to Explore

Write a question related to the data table that you have not yet answered. Then create a graph or work with the data in other ways to answer your question.

Fighting Disease · *Laboratory Investigation*

Do Mouthwashes Work?

Pre-Lab Discussion

What do you use to take care of your teeth: toothbrush, toothpaste, dental floss, mouthwash? Mouthwashes are supposed to kill microorganisms that contribute to tooth decay, gum disease, and bad breath. They contain antiseptics, chemicals that kill or prevent growth of disease organisms on living tissues. How well do these mouthwashes work? Do they really kill microorganisms?

In this investigation, you will compare the effects of two mouthwashes.

1. Name four groups of organisms that cause diseases.

   _____

   _____

2. From where do disease-causing microorganisms come?

   _____

   _____

Problem

How well do mouthwashes control the growth of bacteria?

Materials *(per group)*

3 petri dishes with sterile nutrient agar

pen

masking tape

2 types of mouthwash

2 small jars

filter paper

scissors

metric ruler

forceps

transparent tape

Safety 🗑 🧹 *Review the safety guidelines in Appendix A of your textbook.*

Do not drink the mouthwashes. Have the teacher dispose of the sealed petri dishes at the end of the activity.

Name _____ Date _____ Class _____

Fighting Disease ▪ *Laboratory Investigation*

Procedure

1. Obtain three petri dishes containing sterile agar. Do *not* open the dishes. Using a pen and pieces of masking tape, label the bottoms of the petri dishes A, B, and C. Also put your initials on each dish.

2. Wash your hands thoroughly with soap, then run a fingertip across the surface of your worktable. Your partner should hold open the cover of petri dish A, while you run your fingertip gently across the agar in a zigzag motion. Close the dish immediately.

3. Repeat Step 2 for dishes B and C.

4. Obtain a small sample of each mouthwash in separate containers. Use a pen and masking tape to label the containers.

5. Cut two 2-cm squares of filter paper. Soak a square in each mouthwash.

6. Using forceps, remove one square from a container. Open the cover of dish A just long enough to put the filter paper in the center of the agar. Close the cover immediately. Record the name of the mouthwash in the Data Table.

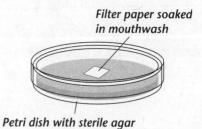

Filter paper soaked in mouthwash

Petri dish with sterile agar

7. Repeat Step 6 for dish B, using the filter paper soaked in the second mouthwash.

8. Do not add anything to dish C.

9. Tape the covers of all three petri dishes so that they will remain tightly closed. Let the three dishes sit upright on your work surface for at least 5 minutes before moving them. **CAUTION:** *Do not open the petri dishes again.* Wash your hands with soap and water.

10. As directed by the teacher, store the petri dishes in a warm, dark place where they can remain for at least three days. You will remove them only for a brief examination each day.

11. Predict what you will observe over the next three days in the three petri dishes.

_____

_____

_____

12. After one day, observe the contents of each dish without removing the cover. Estimate the percentage of the agar surface that shows any changes. Record your observations in the Data Table. Return the dishes to their storage place and wash your hands with soap and water.

13. Repeat Step 12 after a second day and after a third day.

14. After you and your partner have made your last observations, give the unopened petri dishes to the teacher.

Fighting Disease ▪ *Laboratory Investigation*

Do Mouthwashes Work? *(continued)*

Observations

Data Table

Petri Dish	Mouthwash	Day 1	Day 2	Day 3
A				
B				
C				

Analyze and Conclude

1. How did the appearance of dish C change during three days?

   _____

2. How did the appearance of dishes A and B compare with dish C? Explain any similarities or differences.

   _____

   _____

   _____

3. How did the appearance of dishes A and B compare with each other? How can you account for any differences?

   _____

   _____

   _____

4. Explain why it is important to set aside one petri dish that does not contain any mouthwash.

   _____

   _____

   _____

Fighting Disease · *Laboratory Investigation*

Critical Thinking and Applications

1. Based on the results of this lab, what recommendation would you make to your family about mouthwashes?

   _____

   _____

   _____

2. What other products could you test using a procedure similar to this lab?

   _____

   _____

More to Explore

Test one of the products in your answer to question 2 above. For example, visit a store and look at antibacterial soaps. How do their ingredients differ from other soaps? How do their prices compare to regular soap?

_____

_____

New Problem How well do antibacterial soaps control the growth of bacteria?

Possible Materials Consider which materials you can use from the previous part of this lab. What else will you need?

Procedure Develop a procedure to solve the problem. Write your procedure on a separate sheet of paper. Have the teacher approve your procedure before you carry out the investigation.

Observations On a separate sheet of paper, make a data table like the one in the previous part of this lab in which to record your data.

Analyze and Conclude What effects of antibacterial soap do your results show?

_____

_____

_____

The Nervous System • *Design Your Own Lab*

Ready or Not!

Problem

Do people's reaction times vary at different times of day?

Skills Focus

developing hypotheses, controlling variables, drawing conclusions

Material

meter stick

Procedure

PART 1 Observing a Response to a Stimulus

1. Have your partner hold a meter stick with the zero end about 50 cm above a table.

2. Get ready to catch the meter stick by positioning the top of your thumb and forefinger just at the zero position as shown in the diagram.

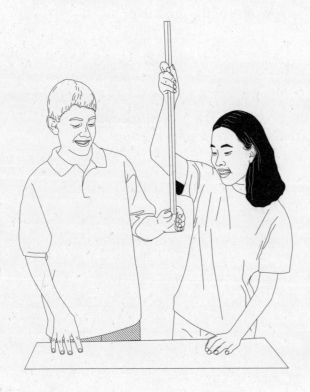

The Nervous System ▪ *Design Your Own Lab*

3. Your partner should drop the meter stick without any warning. Using your thumb and forefinger only (no other part of your hand), catch the meter stick as soon as you can. Record the distance in centimeters that the meter stick fell. This distance is a measure of your reaction time.

PART 2 Designing Your Experiment

4. With your partner, discuss how you can use the activity from Part 1 to find out whether people's reaction times vary at different times of day. Consider the questions below. Then, write up your experimental plan on a separate sheet of paper.

   ▪ What hypothesis will you test?

   ▪ What variables do you need to control?

   ▪ How many people will you test? How many times will you test each person?

5. Submit your plan for your teacher's review. Make any changes your teacher recommends. Create a data table to record your results. Then perform your experiment.

Analyze and Conclude

Write your answers on a separate sheet of paper.

1. **Inferring** In this lab, what is the stimulus? What is the response? Is the response voluntary or involuntary? Explain.
2. **Developing Hypotheses** What hypothesis did you test in Part 2?
3. **Controlling Variables** In Part 2, why was it important to control all variables except the time of day?
4. **Drawing Conclusions** Based on your results in Part 2, do people's reaction times vary at different times of the day? Explain.
5. **Communicating** Write a paragraph to explain why you can use the distance on the meter stick as a measure of reaction time.

More to Explore

Do you think people can do arithmetic problems more quickly and accurately at certain times of the day? Design an experiment to investigate this question. *Obtain your teacher's permission before carrying out your investigation.*

The Nervous System • *Consumer Lab*

With Caffeine or Without?

Problem

What body changes does caffeine produce in blackworms (*Lumbriculus*)?

Skills Focus

observing, controlling variables, drawing conclusions

Materials

blackworms

plastic dropper

adrenaline solution

stereomicroscope

paraffin specimen trough

noncarbonated spring water

beverages with and without caffeine

stopwatch or clock with second hand

Procedure 🫁 🧑‍🔬 🧤 🐁 🔪 **PART 1 Observing the Effects of a Known Stimulant**

1. Use a dropper to remove one worm and a drop or two of water from the blackworm population provided by your teacher.
2. Place the worm and the water in the trough of a paraffin block. Use the dropper or the corner of a paper towel to remove any excess water that does not fit in the trough. Let the blackworm adjust to the block for a few minutes.
3. Place the paraffin block under the stereomicroscope. Select the smallest amount of light and the lowest possible power to view the blackworm.
4. Look through the stereomicroscope and locate a segment near the middle of the worm. Count the number of times blood pulses through this segment for 30 seconds. Multiply this number by two to get the pulse in beats per minute. Record the pulse in the table on the following page.
5. Remove the block from the stereomicroscope. Use the dropper to add 1 drop of adrenaline solution to the trough. (Adrenaline is a substance that is produced by the human body that acts as a stimulant.) Let the worm sit in the adrenaline solution for 5 minutes.

The Nervous System · *Consumer Lab*

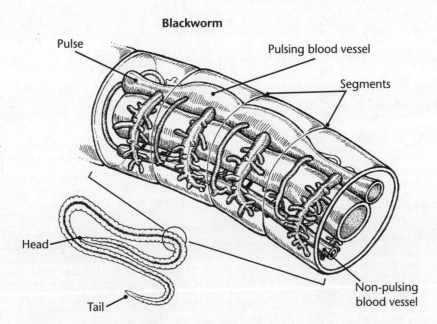

Blackworm

Pulse

Pulsing blood vessel

Segments

Head

Tail

Non-pulsing blood vessel

6. Place the paraffin block under the stereomicroscope. Again locate a segment near the middle of the worm. Count the number of pulses through this segment for 30 seconds. Multiply this number by two to get the pulse in beats per minute. In the data table below, record the blackworm's pulse with adrenaline.

PART 2 Testing the Effects of Caffeine

7. Using the procedures you followed in Part 1, design an experiment that tests the effect of caffeine on the blackworm's pulse. You can use beverages with and without caffeine in your investigation. Be sure to write a hypothesis and control all necessary variables.

8. Submit your experimental plan to your teacher for review. After making any necessary changes, carry out your experiment.

Data Table	
Condition	**Pulse Rate**
No adrenaline	
With adrenaline	
Beverage without caffeine	
Beverage with caffeine	

The Nervous System • *Consumer Lab*

With Caffeine or Without? *(continued)*

Analyze and Conclude

Write your answers on a separate sheet of paper.

1. **Observing** In Part 1, what was the blackworm's pulse rate before you added adrenaline? After you added adrenaline?

   _____

   _____

   _____

2. **Interpreting Data** Use the data you collected in Part 1 to explain how you know that adrenaline acts as a stimulant.

   _____

   _____

   _____

3. **Controlling Variables** In the experiment you performed in Part 2, what was your control? Explain.

   _____

   _____

   _____

4. **Drawing Conclusions** Based on your results in Part 2, does caffeine act as a stimulant? Explain your answer.

   _____

   _____

   _____

5. **Communicating** Write a paragraph to explain how you think your body would react to drinks with and without caffeine. Use the results from this investigation to support your viewpoint.

   _____

   _____

   _____

Design an Experiment

Do you think that "decaffeinated" products will act as a stimulant in blackworms? Design a controlled experiment to find out. *Obtain your teacher's permission before carrying out your investigation.*

The Nervous System · *Laboratory Investigation*

Locating Touch Receptors

Pre-Lab Discussion

Have you ever wondered why your hand instantly pulls back when it touches a hot pan on the stove? Have you noticed that smooth fabrics feel better to your skin than rough fabrics do? Both of these reactions involve your sense of touch.

Touch receptors in your skin help you respond to your environment. Your body responds to different stimuli, including pain, temperature, and pressure. Not all parts of your body respond equally to these stimuli. Different parts of the body contain different numbers of receptors for a given amount of skin area.

In this investigation, you will test several areas of your skin and compare their sensitivity to touch.

1. How does the location of the sense of touch differ from the location of other senses?

   _____

   _____

2. Where in the skin are the receptors that would sense a light touch?

   _____

   _____

Problem

Where are the touch receptors located on the body?

Materials *(per group)*

scissors

metric ruler

piece of cardboard, 6 cm × 10 cm

marker

9 toothpicks

blindfold

Safety *Review the safety guidelines in Appendix A of your textbook.*

Use caution in handling sharp scissors. Tie the blindfold loosely, using special care if the blindfolded student is wearing contact lenses. Students who wear eyeglasses should remove them before wearing a blindfold.

The Nervous System • *Laboratory Investigation*

Locating Touch Receptors *(continued)*

Procedure

1. Using scissors, cut the piece of cardboard into five rectangles, each measuring 6 cm × 2 cm. Label the pieces A–E.

2. As shown in Figure 1, insert two toothpicks 5 mm apart into rectangle A. Insert two toothpicks 1 cm apart into rectangle B, two toothpicks 2 cm apart into rectangle C, and two toothpicks 3 cm apart into rectangle D. In the center of rectangle E, insert one toothpick.

3. Carefully blindfold your partner.

4. Using one of the rectangles, carefully touch the palm side of your partner's fingertip with the ends of the toothpicks.

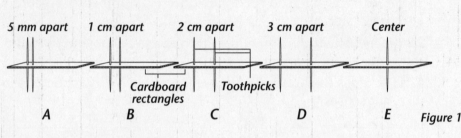

Figure 1

CAUTION: *Only touch the toothpicks to the skin; do not press them against the skin.*

5. In Data Table 1, record how many points your partner felt.

6. Repeat steps 4 and 5, touching the palm of the hand, back of the hand, back of the neck, and inside the lower arm.

7. Repeat steps 4–6 with the other cardboard rectangles. Select each rectangle randomly, not in alphabetical order.

8. Reverse roles with your partner and repeat the investigation using Data Table 2.

9. Answer question 1 in Observations.

Observations

Data Table 1

Body Part	Number of Points Felt				
	A 5 mm apart	**B** 1 cm apart	**C** 2 cm apart	**D** 3 cm apart	**E** 1 point
Subject 1					
Fingertip					
Palm of hand					
Back of hand					
Back of neck					
Inside lower arm					

The Nervous System · *Laboratory Investigation*

Data Table 2

Body Part	Number of Points Felt				
	A *5 mm apart*	*B* *1 cm apart*	*C* *2 cm apart*	*D* *3 cm apart*	*E* *1 point*
Subject 2					
Fingertip					
Palm of hand					
Back of hand					
Back of neck					
Inside lower arm					

1. On which area of the skin were you best able to feel two separate points?

   _____

Analyze and Conclude

1. Which area of the skin that you tested probably had the most touch receptors? The fewest? On what observations do you base this conclusion?

   _____

   _____

   _____

2. Rank the tested skin areas in order from the most to the least sensitive.

   _____

   _____

   _____

3. In Step 7, why was it important to select each rectangle randomly instead of in alphabetical order?

   _____

   _____

   _____

The Nervous System ▪ *Laboratory Investigation*

Locating Touch Receptors *(continued)*

4. Did you and your partner sense the same number of points in each test? If not, why do you think your results were different?

_____

_____

_____

Critical Thinking and Applications

1. Think about the test area that had the most touch receptors. How does having a lot of receptors in this area benefit you?

_____

_____

_____

2. Explain how a lack of touch receptors in the bottom of your feet would affect your ability to walk.

_____

_____

_____

3. Why is it important to you that your body respond to pain?

_____

_____

More to Explore

New Problem Can you identify similar objects by touch alone?

Possible Materials Consider which materials you can use from the previous part of the lab. What else will you need?

Procedure Develop a procedure to solve the problem. Write your procedure on a separate sheet of paper. Have the teacher approve your procedure before you carry out the investigation.

Observations On a separate sheet of paper, create a table to organize data for two subjects trying to identify three coins each.

Analyze and Conclude Do different people have different touch sensitivity? Support your answer with data from your experiment.

_____

_____

The Endocrine System and Reproduction · *Technology Lab*

Modeling Negative Feedback

Problem

How can you model negative feedback?

Skills Focus

observing, making models, evaluating the design

Materials

duct tape

round balloon

scissors

rubber stopper

string, 40 cm

large plastic soda bottle (2 L) with bottom removed

small plastic soda bottle (1 L)

plastic tray

water

Procedure

PART 1 Research and Investigate

1. The diagram below shows how a flush toilet uses negative feedback to regulate the water level. In your notebook, describe which part of the process involves negative feedback.

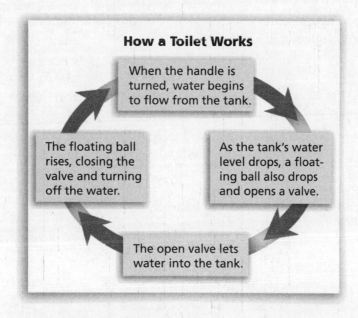

How a Toilet Works

When the handle is turned, water begins to flow from the tank.

As the tank's water level drops, a floating ball also drops and opens a valve.

The open valve lets water into the tank.

The floating ball rises, closing the valve and turning off the water.

The Endocrine System and Reproduction • *Technology Lab*

Modeling Negative Feedback *(continued)*

PART 2 Design and Build

2. As you hold the open end of a balloon, push its closed end through the mouth of a small plastic bottle. Do not push the open end of the balloon into the bottle. Then, slide a straw part way into the bottle so that the air inside the bottle can escape as you blow up the balloon.

3. Partially blow up the balloon inside the bottle. The partially inflated balloon should be about the size of a tennis ball. Remove the straw. Tie the balloon tightly, then push it into the bottle.

4. Place the large plastic bottle mouth to mouth with the small bottle. Tape the two bottles together. Make sure that the seal is waterproof.

5. Tie one end of a piece of string around the top of a rubber stopper.

6. Place the attached bottles on the tray with the smaller bottle on the bottom. Place the stopper loosely into the mouth of the larger bottle.

7. While one partner holds the bottles upright, add water to the large bottle until it is about three fourths full. Then gently pull the string to remove the stopper. Watch what happens. Pay close attention to the following: What does the balloon do as water rises in the small bottle? Does the small bottle completely fill with water? Record your observations.

8. In your notebook, record which part of your device models negative feedback.

Analyze and Conclude

1. **Inferring** Summarize your research from Part 1 by describing an example of negative feedback.

2. **Observing** Describe the events you observed in Step 7.

3. **Making Models** In Step 7, which part of the process involves negative feedback? Explain your answer.

4. **Evaluating the Design** Suggest one way you could change the model to show that negative feedback can be part of a cycle.

Communicating

Suppose you are a TV health reporter preparing a program on human hormones. You need to do a 30-second segment on hormones and negative feedback. Write a script for your presentation. Include references to a model to help viewers understand how negative feedback works in the endocrine system.

The Endocrine System and Reproduction • *Skills Lab*

Growing Up

Problem

How do the proportions of the human body change during development?

Skills Focus

calculating, predicting

Procedure

1. Examine the diagram below. Notice that the figures are drawn against a graph showing percentages. You can use this diagram to determine how the lengths of major body parts compare to each figure's height. Use the data table on the next page to record information about each figure's head size and leg length.

2. Look at Figure D. You can use the graph to estimate that the head is about 15 percent of the figure's full height. Record that number in your data table.

3. Examine Figures A through C. Determine the percentage of the total height that the head makes up. Record your results.

4. Now compare the length of the legs to the total body height for Figures A through D. Record your results. (*Hint:* Figure A shows the legs folded. You will need to estimate the data for that figure.)

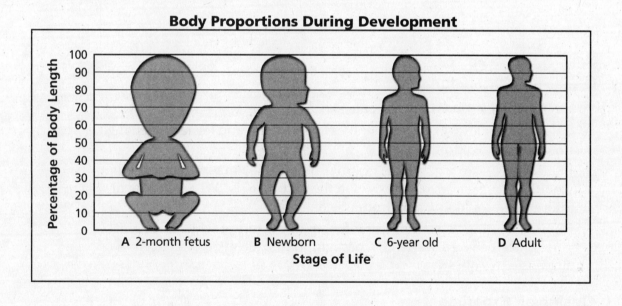

Body Proportions During Development

The Endocrine System and Reproduction • *Skills Lab*

Growing Up *(continued)*

Data Table

	Head Size	Leg Length
Figure A		
Figure B		
Figure C		
Figure D		

Analyze and Conclude

Answer these questions on a separate sheet of paper.

1. **Calculating** How do the percentages for head size and leg length change from infancy to adulthood?

2. **Predicting** If you made a line graph using the data in the diagram, what would be on the horizontal axis? On the vertical axis? What additional information could you gain from this line graph?

3. **Communicating** What can you infer about the rate at which different parts of the body grow? Write a paragraph in which you discuss the answer to this question.

Design an Experiment

Make a prediction about the relationship between the circumference of the head and body height. Then design an experiment to test your prediction, using people for test subjects. *Obtain your teacher's permission before carrying out your investigation.*

The Endocrine System and Reproduction ▪ *Laboratory Investigation*

Model of a Negative Feedback Mechanism

Pre-Lab Discussion

The endocrine system, along with the nervous system, controls your body's daily activities. It also controls how your body develops. Endocrine glands produce chemicals called hormones, which move directly into the bloodstream. Hormones affect specific cells called target cells. These target cells are often in another part of the body. To control the amount of hormone an endocrine gland produces, the endocrine system sends chemical information back and forth in a negative feedback system. Negative feedback is an important way that the body maintains homeostasis. In this investigation, you will model how a negative feedback system works.

1. How does the pancreas act as an endocrine gland?

_____

_____

2. Your blood carries hormones to every part of your body. Why doesn't a hormone affect all your cells the same way?

_____

_____

_____

Problem

How does the pancreas use negative feedback to help maintain glucose at a certain level in the blood?

Materials *(per group)*

2-liter plastic soft-drink bottle

scissors

rubber ball, solid, 2.5-4.0 cm in diameter

2 screw eyes

string

fishing float

dowel, about 6 cm long

sink or bucket

water

large pitcher

marker

The Endocrine System and Reproduction • *Laboratory Investigation*

Model of a Negative Feedback Mechanism *(continued)*

Safety

 Review the safety guidelines in Appendix A of your textbook.

Take care when cutting off the bottom of the soft-drink bottle. To prevent slips or falls, immediately wipe up any water spilled on the floor.

Procedure

1. Carefully cut off the bottom half of the plastic bottle.

2. Insert a screw eye into a rubber ball. Cut a piece of string 20 cm long. Tie one end of the string to the screw eye and the other end to a fishing float.

3. Insert a second screw eye into the other side of the rubber ball, directly opposite the first screw eye. Cut a piece of string 10 cm long. Tie one end of the string to the screw eye and the other end to the middle of the dowel.

4. Hold the bottle upside down. Lower the float, the rubber ball, and the attached dowel into the bottle. Carefully pass the dowel through the neck of the bottle so that the dowel hangs below the mouth, as shown in Figure 1.

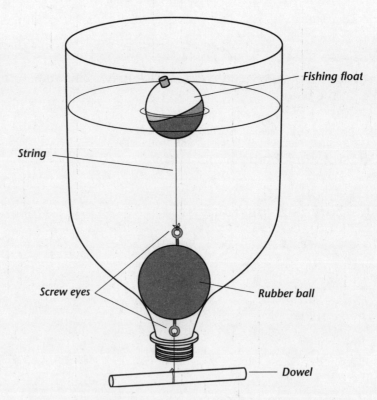

Figure 1
(Not drawn to scale)

Fishing float

String

Screw eyes

Rubber ball

Dowel

5. One of you should hold the bottle over a sink or bucket, while the other slowly pours water into the bottle until the string stretches to its full length. Do not lift the ball out of the bottle opening. Mark the level of the water on the outside of the bottle.

The Endocrine System and Reproduction • *Laboratory Investigation*

6. Slowly add more water to the bottle and observe what happens. Answer questions 1 and 2 in Observations.

7. Add about 100 mL of water rapidly to the model. Be careful not to overfill the bottle. Observe what happens and answer question 3 in Observations.

Observations

1. What happens to the water level when you add more water after the string has stretched to its full length?

_____

_____

_____

_____

_____

2. What happens to the float and ball whenever you add water slowly?

_____

_____

_____

_____

_____

3. How does the model act when you pour the water quickly, compared to when you pour it slowly?

_____

_____

_____

_____

_____

Analyze and Conclude

Figure 2 on the next page shows the role of the pancreas in a negative feedback loop that controls the amount of glucose in the blood. The pancreas makes the hormone insulin. Insulin enables body cells to take in glucose from the bloodstream. When the glucose level in the blood is high, the pancreas releases insulin, which enables body cells to take glucose from the blood. When the glucose level in the blood drops, the pancreas stops releasing insulin. Body cells stop removing glucose from the bloodstream. When blood glucose increases, the cycle starts again.

The Endocrine System and Reproduction • *Laboratory Investigation*

Model of a Negative Feedback Mechanism *(continued)*

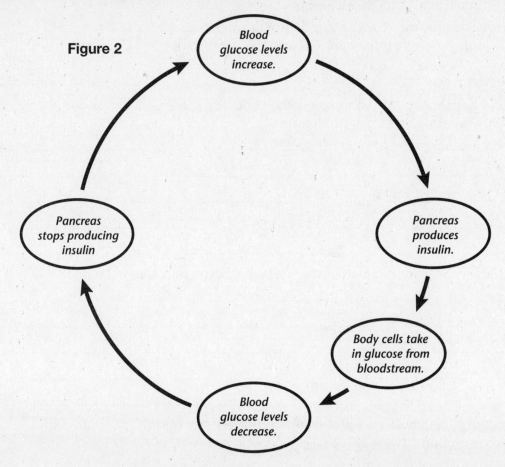

Figure 2

Blood glucose levels increase.

Pancreas produces insulin.

Body cells take in glucose from bloodstream.

Blood glucose levels decrease.

Pancreas stops producing insulin

1. The water in the model represents blood glucose. Which part of your model represents the pancreas? (Drawing a cycle like the one in Figure 2 might help you find an answer.) Give a reason for your answer.

   _____

   _____

   _____

2. Which part of your model represents the body cells? Give a reason for your answer.

   _____

   _____

   _____

3. Which part of your model represents insulin? Give a reason for your answer.

   _____

   _____

   _____

The Endocrine System and Reproduction • *Laboratory Investigation*

4. Explain how your model demonstrates the negative feedback mechanism used by the pancreas to control glucose levels in the blood.

_____

_____

_____

_____

_____

_____

Critical Thinking and Applications

1. How would lengthening the string between the float and the ball affect the water level? How would shortening this string affect the water level?

_____

_____

_____

2. Based on this model, explain how negative feedback works.

_____

_____

_____

_____

3. What part of the negative feedback mechanism that keeps blood glucose at one level is not represented in the model? How could you improve the design of the model to make it more accurate?

_____

_____

_____

_____

_____

More to Explore

The body's regulation of glucose levels is more complicated than the model you made of it. Use the library to find out more about glucose regulation. Which part of the regulation process is missing from your model?

Populations and Communities · *Skills Lab*

A World in a Bottle

Problem

How do organisms survive in a closed ecosystem?

Skills Focus

making models, observing

Materials

pre-cut, clear plastic bottle
gravel
soil
moss plants
plastic spoon
charcoal
spray bottle
large rubber band
2 vascular plants
plastic wrap

Procedure 🔲 🔲 🔲 *Review the safety guidelines in Appendix A.*

1. In this lab, you will place plants in moist soil in a bottle that then will be sealed. This setup is called a terrarium. Predict whether the plants can survive in this habitat.

2. Spread about 2.5 cm of gravel on the bottom of a pre-cut bottle. Then sprinkle a spoonful or two of charcoal over the gravel.

3. Use the spoon to layer about eight cm of soil over the gravel and charcoal. After you add the soil, tap it down to pack it.

4. Scoop out two holes in the soil. Remove the vascular plants from their pots. Gently place their roots in the holes. Then pack the loose soil firmly around the plants' stems.

5. Fill the spray bottle with water. Spray the soil until you see water collecting in the gravel.

6. Cover the soil with the moss plants, including the areas around the stems of the vascular plants. Lightly spray the mosses with water.

7. Tightly cover your terrarium with plastic wrap. Secure the cover with a rubber band. Place the terrarium in bright, indirect sunlight.

8. Observe your terrarium daily for two weeks. Record your observations in your notebook. If its sides fog, move the terrarium to an area with a different amount of light. You may need to move it a few times. Note any changes you make in your terrarium's location.

Populations and Communities • *Skills Lab*

Analyze and Conclude

Write your answers on a separate sheet of paper.

1. **Making Models** List all of the biotic factors and abiotic factors that are part of your ecosystem model.

2. **Observing** Were any biotic or abiotic factors able to enter the terrarium? If so, which ones?

3. **Inferring** Draw a diagram showing the interactions between the terrarium's biotic and abiotic factors.

4. **Predicting** Suppose a plant-eating insect were added to the terrarium. Predict whether it would be able to survive. Explain your prediction.

5. **Communicating** Write a paragraph that explains how your terrarium models an ecosystem on Earth. How does your model differ from that ecosystem?

Design an Experiment

Plan an experiment that would model a freshwater ecosystem. How would this model be different from the land ecosystem? *Obtain your teacher's approval before carrying out your plan.*

Populations and Communities • *Skills Lab*

Counting Turtles

Problem

How can the mark-and-recapture method help ecologists monitor the size of a population?

Skills Focus

calculating, graphing, predicting

Materials

- model paper turtle population
- calculator
- graph paper

Procedure

1. The data table shows the results from the first three years of a study to determine the number of snapping turtles in a pond.

2. Your teacher will give you a box representing the pond. Fifteen of the turtles have been marked, as shown in the data table for Year 4.

3. Capture a member of the population by randomly selecting one turtle. Set it aside.

4. Repeat Step 3 nine times. Record the total number of turtles you captured.

5. Examine each turtle to see whether it has a mark. Count the number of recaptured (marked) turtles. Record this number in the data table.

Data Table

Year	Number Marked	Total Number Captured	Number Recaptured (with Marks)	Estimated Total Population
1	32	28	15	
2	25	21	11	
3	23	19	11	
4	15			

Populations and Communities ▪ *Skills Lab*

Analyze and Conclude

Write your answers in the spaces provided.

1. **Calculating** Use the equation below to estimate the turtle population for each year. The first year is done for you as a sample. Write your calculations on a separate sheet of paper. If your answer is a decimal, round it to the nearest whole number. Record the population for each year in the last column of the data table.

$$\text{Total population} = \frac{\text{Number marked} \times \text{Total number captured}}{\text{Number recaptured (with marks)}}$$

Sample (Year 1):

$$32 \times \frac{28}{15} = 59.7 \text{ or } 60 \text{ turtles}$$

2. **Graphing** On the next page, graph the estimated total populations for the four years. Mark years on the horizontal axis. Mark population size on the vertical axis.

3. **Interpreting Data** Describe how the turtle population has changed over the four years of the study. Suggest three possible causes for the changes.

_____

_____

_____

_____

_____

4. **Predicting** Use your graph to predict what the turtle population will be in Year 5. Explain your prediction.

_____

_____

_____

_____

5. **Communicating** Write a paragraph that explains why the mark-and-recapture method is a useful tool for ecologists. When is this technique most useful for estimating population size?

_____

_____

_____

_____

Populations and Communities ▪ *Skills Lab*

Counting Turtles (continued)

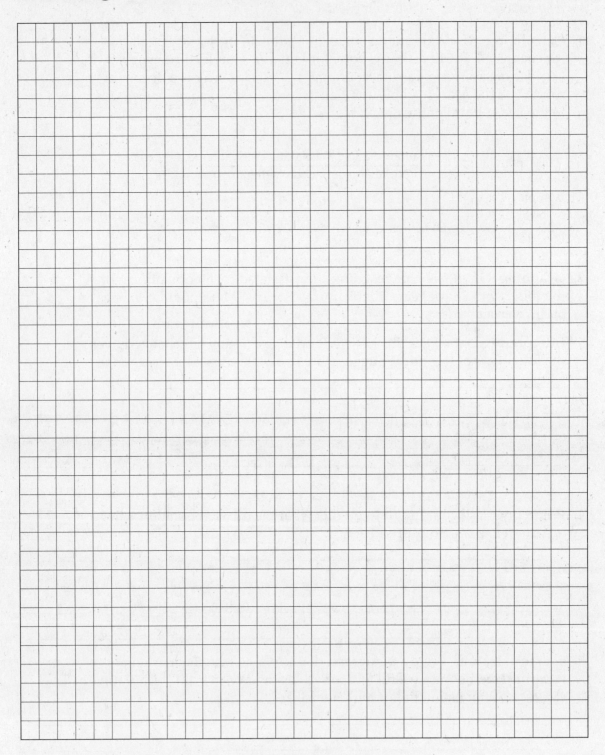

More to Explore

Suppose that only six turtles had been recaptured in Year 2. How would this change your graph?

Name _____ Date _____ Class _____

Populations and Communities · *Laboratory Investigation*

Weather and Whooping Cranes

Pre-Lab Discussion

The whooping crane is a tall, white bird with red markings on its forehead and face. It is native to certain North American wetlands. In the 1900s, the population of this magnificent bird had decreased almost to the point of disappearing. In 1941, only 14 cranes were living. Although more than ten times as many cranes are now living in the wild, they are still at risk. About half of the cranes live in the wild. Most breed in Wood Buffalo National Park in Canada and winter in Aransas National Wildlife Refuge in Texas.

Scientists, working to save the whooping cranes, investigated what abiotic factors affect the birds. In this investigation, you will analyze the data from one such study.

1. What do whooping cranes need to obtain from their habitat?

   _____

   _____

2. What abiotic factors might limit the population of whooping cranes?

   _____

   _____

Problem

How does precipitation affect the population of whooping cranes?

Materials *(per group)*

ruler

calculator

pencil

Procedure

1. Using Figure 1 and the data in Data Table 1, plot a graph showing how the crane population changed from year 1 to year 16 of the study. The crane population in any given year is the total number of migrating adults and hatched eggs. Answer Questions 1–2 in Observations.

2. Study the data in Data Table 1. Answer Questions 3–6 in Observations.

3. Using a calculator, determine the hatching success rate for each year.

$$\text{Hatching success rate} = \frac{\text{Number of eggs hatched}}{\text{Number of eggs laid}} \times 100\%$$

Write these values in the corresponding boxes in Data Table 2. Answer Question 7 in Observations.

Populations and Communities ▪ *Laboratory Investigation*

Weather and Whooping Cranes *(continued)*

Data Table 1

One Study Relating Weather and Reproductive Rate of Whooping Cranes

Year	Migrating Adults	Number of Nests	Eggs Laid	Hatched Eggs	Rainfall (cm)	Snowfall (cm)
1	21	6	6	4	8.9	3.6
2	20	3	2	0	15.0	0.5
3	20	4	4	3	11.7	2.0
4	22	5	5	4	6.1	2.8
5	23	4	6	2	6.4	14.2
6	23	8	8	4	8.1	4.6
7	30	6	6	5	7.4	0.0
8	32	0	0	0	19.3	7.6
9	28	4	6	2	15.0	1.3
10	26	10	10	7	8.1	2.0
11	32	10	10	6	7.4	2.5
12	36	2	2	0	13.7	7.4
13	30	4	4	3	8.9	1.0
14	32	3	4	3	7.1	1.8
15	33	3	3	1	14.7	6.1
16	32	5	5	4	5.3	1.5

Populations and Communities • *Laboratory Investigation*

Observations

Figure 1

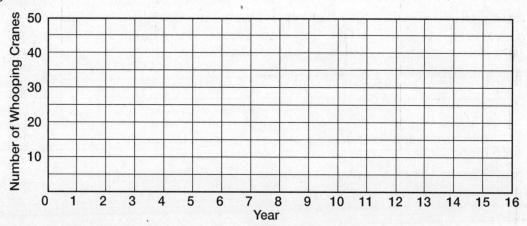

1. When was the crane population at its highest level? When was it at its lowest level?

   _____

2. During which year did the population increase the most?

   _____

3. In which year did the most adult cranes die?

   _____

4. Which four years were the poorest breeding years for the cranes? In which year were the most eggs laid and hatched successfully?

   _____

   _____

5. During which five summers was rainfall greatest?

   _____

6. Was snowfall ever high the same year that rainfall was high? If so, in which year or years?

   _____

7. In which year was total precipitation (rainfall plus snowfall) lowest? What was the hatching success rate that year?

   _____

Data Table 2

Year	1	2	3	4	5	6	7	8	9	10	11	12	13	14	15	16
Hatching Success Rate (%)																

Populations and Communities • *Laboratory Investigation*

Weather and Whooping Cranes (continued)

Analyze and Conclude

1. Using data from data tables 1 and 2, plot the points that relate hatching success rate to rainfall on Figure 2 below. What is the relationship between rainfall and hatching success rate? Why do you think this relationship exists?

_____

_____

_____

_____

Figure 2

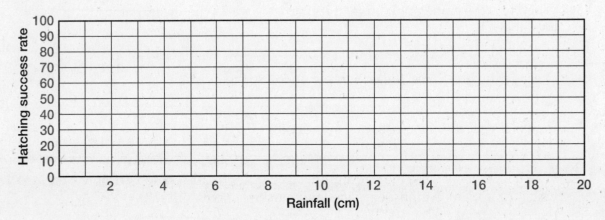

2. Suppose you want to find out how rainfall affects the whooping-crane population. Why would you need to find daily or weekly amounts of rainfall rather than seasonal amounts?

_____

_____

_____

3. Suppose that years 10 and 11 had high levels of precipitation. How would this have affected the population? Give a reason for your answer.

_____

_____

_____

_____

Populations and Communities ▪ *Laboratory Investigation*

Critical Thinking and Applications

1. What other factors besides weather might influence the population growth of whooping cranes? What do you think lowered the whooping-crane population to the endangered level?

   _____

   _____

   _____

2. Once laws protecting the American alligator went into effect, the alligator population recovered quite rapidly. In contrast, the whooping-crane population has remained low in spite of protection. What factors might prevent a rapid increase in the number of cranes?

   _____

   _____

   _____

3. Why is international cooperation necessary to protect species that migrate, such as the whooping crane?

   _____

   _____

   _____

4. Whooping cranes often lay two eggs. However, a pair can rarely raise two chicks. Therefore, wildlife biologists sometimes "steal" one of the two eggs in the nest and replace it with a fake one of plastic. What do you think the biologists do with the stolen eggs? Why?

   _____

   _____

   _____

More to Explore

Find out the difference between an endangered species and a threatened species. Is the whooping crane endangered or threatened? List three species that are endangered and three species that are threatened. What is being done to protect each species?

Ecosystems and Biomes ▪ *Skills Lab*

Biomes in Miniature

Problem

What biotic and abiotic factors create different biomes around the world?

Skills Focus

observing, making models

Materials

scissors

clear plastic wrap

index card

lamp

tape

empty, clean cardboard milk carton

stapler

about 30 rye grass seeds

10 impatiens seeds

5 lima bean seeds

sandy soil or potting soil

Procedure *Review the safety guidelines in Appendix A.*

1. Your teacher will assign your group a biome. You will also observe the other groups' model biomes. Based on the chart on the next page, predict how well you think each of the three kinds of seeds will grow in each set of conditions. Record these predictions in your notebook. Then copy the data table on the next page four times, once for each biome.

2. Staple the spout of the milk carton closed. Completely cut away one of the four sides of the carton. Poke a few holes in the opposite side for drainage, and then place that side down.

3. Fill the carton to 3 centimeters from the top with the type of soil given in the table. Divide the surface of the soil into three sections by making two lines in it with a pencil.

4. In the section near the spout, plant the impatiens seeds. In the middle section, plant the lima bean seeds. In the third section, scatter the rye grass seeds on the surface.

5. Water all the seeds well. Then cover the open part of the carton with plastic wrap.

6. On an index card, write the name of your biome, the names of the three types of seeds in the order you planted them, and the names of your group members. Tape the card to the carton. Put the carton in a warm place where it will not be disturbed.

Name _____ Date _____ Class _____

Ecosystems and Biomes ▪ *Skills Lab*

7. Once the seeds sprout, provide your biome with light and water as specified in the chart. Keep the carton covered with plastic wrap except when you add water.

8. Observe all the model biomes daily for at least one week. Record your observations.

Growing Conditions			
Biome	**Soil Type**	**Hours of Light per Day**	**Watering Instructions**
Forest	Potting soil	1–2 hours of direct light	Let the surface dry; then add water.
Desert	Sandy soil	5–6 hours of direct light	Let the soil dry to a depth of 2.5 cm below the surface
Grassland	Potting soil	5–6 hours of direct light	Let the surface dry; then add water.
Rain forest	Potting soil	No direct light; indirect light for 5–6 hours	Keep the surface of the soil moist.

Data Table			
Name of biome:			
Day	*Impatiens*	*Lima Beans*	*Rye Grass*
1			
2			
3			
4			
5			
6			
7			

Ecosystems and Biomes · *Skills Lab*

Biomes in Miniature *(continued)*

Analyze and Conclude

Answer the following questions in the spaces provided.

1. **Observing** In which model biome did each type of seed grow best? In which model biome did each type of seed grow least well?

   _____
   _____
   _____

2. **Making Models** In this experiment, how did you model the following abiotic factors: sunlight, water, and temperature?

   _____
   _____
   _____

3. **Inferring** How was each type of seed affected by the soil type, amount of light, and availability of water?

   _____
   _____
   _____

4. **Classifying** Why do you think that ecologists who study biomes often focus on identifying the key abiotic factors and typical plants in an area?

   _____
   _____
   _____

5. **Communicating** Write a paragraph explaining how your miniature biomes modeled real-life biomes. Which features of real-life biomes were you able to model well? Which features of real-life biomes were more difficult to model?

   _____
   _____
   _____

Design an Experiment

Write a plan for setting up a model rain forest or desert terrarium. Include typical plants found in that biome. *Obtain your teacher's approval before carrying out your investigation.*

Ecosystems and Biomes · *Skills Lab*

Change in a Tiny Community

Problem

How does a pond community change over time?

Skills Focus

observing, classifying

Materials

hay solution

pond water

small baby-food jar

wax pencil

plastic dropper

microscope slide

coverslip

microscope

Procedure *Review the safety guidelines in Appendix A.*

1. Use a wax pencil to label a small jar with your name.

2. Fill the jar about three-fourths full with hay solution. Add pond water until the jar is nearly full. Examine the mixture, and record your observations in your notebook.

3. Place the jar in a safe location out of direct sunlight where it will remain undisturbed. Wash your hands thoroughly with soap after handling the jar or its contents.

4. After two days, examine the contents of the jar, and record your observations.

5. Use a plastic dropper to collect a few drops from the surface of the solution in the jar. Make a slide following the procedures in the box. **CAUTION:** *Slides and coverslips are fragile, and their edges are sharp. Handle them carefully.*

6. Examine the slide under a microscope using both low and high power, following the procedures in your textbook. Draw each type of organism you observe. Estimate the number of each type in your sample. The illustration on the next page shows some of the organisms you might see.

7. Repeat Steps 5 and 6 with a drop of solution taken from the side of the jar beneath the surface.

8. Repeat Steps 5 and 6 with a drop of solution taken from the bottom of the jar. When you are finished, follow your teacher's directions about cleaning up.

9. After 3 days, repeat Steps 5 through 8.

10. After 3 more days, repeat Steps 5 through 8 again. Then follow your teacher's directions for returning the solution.

Ecosystems and Biomes · *Skills Lab*

Change in a Tiny Community *(continued)*

Making and Viewing a Slide

A. Place one drop of the solution to be examined on a microscope slide. Place one edge of a coverslip at the edge of the drop. Gently lower the coverslip over the drop. Try not to trap any air bubbles.

B. Place the slide on the stage of a microscope so the drop is over the opening in the stage. Adjust the stage clips to hold the slide.

C. Look from the side of the microscope, and use the coarse adjustment knob to move the low-power objective close to, but not touching, the coverslip.

D. Look through the eyepiece, and use the coarse adjustment knob to raise the body tube and bring the slide into view. Use the fine adjustment knob to bring the slide into focus.

E. To view the slide under high power, look from the side of the microscope, and revolve the nosepiece until the high-power objective clicks into place just over, but not touching, the slide.

F. While you are looking through the eyepiece, use the fine adjustment knob to bring the slide into focus.

Analyze and Conclude

Answer the following items on a separate sheet.

1. **Classifying** Identify as many of the organisms you observed as possible. Use the diagrams on this page and any other resources your teacher provides.

2. **Observing** How did the community change over the time that you made your observations?

3. **Inferring** What biotic and abiotic factors may have influenced the changes in this community? Explain.

4. **Developing Hypotheses** Where did the organisms you observed in the jar come from?

5. **Communicating** Based on your observations in this lab, write a paragraph that explains why ecosystems change gradually over time. Discuss the important factors that lead to changes in ecosystems.

Daphnia

Paramecium

Design an Experiment

Write a hypothesis about what would happen if you changed one biotic or abiotic factor in this activity. Design a plan to test your hypothesis. *Obtain your teacher's permission before carrying out your investigation.*

Spirogyra

Ecosystems and Biomes ▪ *Laboratory Investigation*

Ecosystem Food Chains

Pre-Lab Discussion

Ecosystems are made up of both living (biotic) and nonliving (abiotic) things. Energy moves through ecosystems in the form of food. When an organism eats another organism, it obtains energy from the food. A food chain is a series of events in which one organism eats another and thereby obtains energy.

Do you know what makes up the ecosystems in your area? In this investigation, you will become an ecologist studying a local ecosystem. You will observe and collect data about the biotic and abiotic factors found at your site. You will also study the relationships among the different biotic and abiotic features you observe.

1. What is a consumer? What are the four classifications of consumers?

_____

_____

2. What types of organisms are the source of all the food in an ecosystem? What process is generally used to make this food?

_____

_____

Problem

What food chains can you observe in a local ecosystem?

Possible Materials *(per group)*

meter stick
4 stakes
string
notebook
pen
colored pencils
hand lens

Time

two 40-minute classes

Safety 🖐 🐾 🔪 *Review the safety guidelines in Appendix A of your textbook.*

Use care when working with stakes. Be careful when working around land and water sites so that you do not fall and injure yourself or others. Review the Safety Rules in the front of this book for handling plants and animals.

Name _____ Date _____ Class _____

Ecosystems and Biomes · *Laboratory Investigation*

Ecosystem Food Chains (continued)

Procedure
Part A: Class Preparation

1. As a class, discuss the different types of ecosystems found around your home and school. Determine which ecosystem you will examine. Be aware that the type of ecosystem you choose will influence the types of food chains you will find.

2. Use different colored pencils to represent the different types of organisms you expect to find within your chosen ecosystem. Make a key representing the different organisms in the Data Table under Observations. Types of organisms might include trees, bushes, flowers, grasses, mosses, fungi, insects, and other animals. You might also include evidence of animals, such as burrows, nests, and egg cases. Finally, consider including dead organic materials such as logs, dead trees, fallen leaves, and animal remains.

3. Make a list of the materials that you need to conduct your field study of the ecosystem. Develop a plan for gathering these materials. Decide who will gather what materials.

Part B: Field Study

1. At your study site, measure a 25-square-meter site with a meter stick (5 m × 5 m). Place one stake at each corner of the site. Loop string around one stake and continue to the next stake until you have formed the boundaries for the site. See Figure 1.

Figure 1

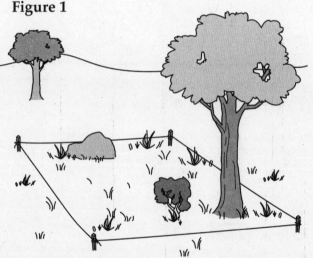

2. On a separate sheet of paper, draw a map of your site. Draw the abiotic features on your map, such as streams, sidewalks, trails, or boulders.

3. Draw colored circles on the map to represent the different organisms you find. Some of your circles will likely overlap. For example, if your site is mostly grass, you may have a colored circle around the entire map. Within this circle might be other colored circles representing trees.

4. Observe your site quietly for 30 minutes. On a separate sheet of paper, record any interactions between organisms that you observe. Such interactions may include getting food or just moving across the site.

5. When you have finished your observations, remove the string and stakes. Leave the site as you found it; do not take anything from it or damage it in any way.

Ecosystems and Biomes · *Laboratory Investigation*

Observations

Data Table			
Color Key for Organisms			
Color	*Type of Organism*	*Color*	*Type of Organism*

Analyze and Conclude

1. What producers did you observe at your site? What characteristics do these organisms have in common?

_____

_____

_____

_____

2. Think about the consumers you observed at your site. Categorize them according to the four main types of consumers that you listed in Pre-Lab Question 1.

_____

_____

_____

_____

3. What are the most important abiotic features of your site? Explain your answer.

_____

_____

_____

_____

Ecosystems and Biomes · *Laboratory Investigation*

Ecosystem Food Chains (continued)

Critical Thinking and Applications

1. Draw two food chains you observed in your site that contain a producer, a primary consumer, and a secondary consumer. Include appropriate organisms in your drawings even if you did not observe the actual consumption of food.

_____

_____

_____

_____

2. How do the abiotic factors in your ecosystem affect how the living things in the ecosystem are distributed?

_____

_____

_____

3. What would happen to the producers and consumers at your site if there were no decomposers?

_____

_____

_____

_____

4. Predict how the biotic and abiotic features might change at your site during different seasons.

_____

_____

_____

_____

More to Explore

Compare your site to other sites nearby. Consider both biotic and abiotic features. Also describe any evidence of human influence on your site.

Living Resources • *Skills Lab*

Recycling Paper

Problem

Is paper a renewable resource?

Skills Focus

observing, predicting

Materials

newspaper

microscope

water

eggbeater

square pan

screen

plastic wrap

mixing bowl

heavy book

microscope slide

Procedure

1. Tear off a small piece of newspaper. Place it on a microscope slide and examine it under a microscope. Record your observations.

2. Tear a sheet of newspaper into pieces about the size of postage stamps. Place the pieces in the mixing bowl. Add enough water to cover the newspaper. Cover the bowl and let the mixture stand overnight.

3. The next day, add more water to cover the paper if necessary. Use the eggbeater to mix the wet paper until it is smooth. This thick liquid is called paper pulp.

4. Place the screen in the bottom of the pan. Pour the pulp onto the screen, spreading it out evenly. Then lift the screen above the pan, allowing most of the water to drip into the pan.

5. Place the screen and pulp on several layers of newspaper to absorb the rest of the water. Lay a sheet of plastic wrap over the pulp. Place a heavy book on top of the plastic wrap to press more water out of the pulp.

6. After 30 minutes, remove the book. Carefully turn over the screen, plastic wrap, and pulp. Remove the screen and plastic wrap. Let the pulp sit on the newspaper for one or two more days to dry. Replace the newspaper layers if necessary.

7. When the pulp is dry, observe it closely. Record your observations.

Living Resources · *Skills Lab*

Recycling Paper *(continued)*

Analyze and Conclude

Write your answers in the spaces provided.

1. **Observing** What kind of structures did you observe when you examined torn newspaper under a microscope?

    _____

    _____

    _____

    _____

2. **Inferring** What are these structures made of? Where do they come from?

    _____

    _____

    _____

3. **Predicting** What do you think happens to those structures you observed when paper is recycled? How do you think this affects the number of times paper can be recycled?

    _____

    _____

    _____

    _____

4. **Communicating** Based on what you learned in this lab, do you think paper should be classified as a renewable or nonrenewable resource? Defend your answer with evidence and sound reasoning.

    _____

    _____

    _____

Living Resources ▪ *Skills Lab*

Design an Experiment

Using procedures like those in this lab, design an experiment to recycle three different types of paper, such as shiny magazine paper, paper towels, and cardboard. *Obtain your teacher's approval for your plans before you try your experiment.* How do the resulting papers differ?

Write your experiment plan below. If you need more room, use a separate sheet of paper.

Hypothesis

_____

_____

_____

_____

_____

Materials

_____

_____

_____

_____

Procedure

_____

_____

_____

_____

_____

_____

_____

_____

_____

_____

_____

Living Resources ▪ *Skills Lab*

Tree Cookie Tales

Problem

What can tree cookies reveal about the past?

Skills Focus

observing, inferring, interpreting data

Materials

tree cookie
metric ruler
hand lens
colored pencils
calculator (optional)

Procedure

1. Your teacher will give you a "tree cookie"—a slice of a tree trunk that contains clues about the tree's age, past weather conditions, and fires that occurred during its life. Use a hand lens to examine your tree cookie. Draw a simple diagram of your tree cookie. Label the bark, tree rings, and center, or pith.

2. Notice the light-colored and dark-colored rings. The light ring results from fast springtime growth. The dark ring, where the cells are smaller, results from slower summertime growth. Each pair of light and dark rings represents one year's growth, so the pair is called an annual ring. Observe and count the annual rings.

   _____

3. Compare the spring and summer portions of the annual rings. Identify the thinnest and thickest rings.

   _____

4. Measure the distance from the center to the outermost edge of the last summer growth ring. This is the radius of your tree cookie. Record your measurement.

   _____

5. Measure the distance from the center to the outermost edge of the tenth summer growth ring. Record your measurement.

   _____

Living Resources ▪ *Skills Lab*

6. Examine your tree cookie for any other evidence of its history, such as
   damaged bark or burn marks. Record your observations.

_____

_____

_____

Analyze and Conclude

Write your answers in the spaces provided.

1. **Inferring** How old was your tree? How do you know?

_____

_____

2. **Calculating** What percent of the tree's growth took place during the first
   ten years of its life? (*Hint:* Divide the distance from the center to the tenth
   growth ring by the radius. Then multiply by 100. This gives you the
   percent of growth that occurred during the tree's first ten years.)

_____

3. **Observing** How did the spring rings compare to the summer rings for
   the same year? Suggest a reason.

_____

_____

4. **Interpreting Data** Why might the annual rings be narrower for some
   years than for others?

_____

5. **Communicating** Using evidence from your tree cookie, write a
   paragraph that summarizes the history of the tree. Be sure to include as
   much detail as possible in your summary.

_____

_____

_____

6. **Design an Experiment** Suppose you had cookies from two other trees of
   the same species that grew near your tree. Write a plan for verifying the
   interpretations you made in this lab. *Obtain your teacher's permission before
   carrying out your investigation.*

_____

_____

_____

Living Resources · *Laboratory Investigation*

Managing Fisheries

Pre-Lab Discussion

When explorers first came to the shores of North America, they were amazed at the abundance of resources—towering forests, clear streams, vast grasslands, and a large variety of wildlife. As they began to use these resources, they also began to affect them. Throughout the years, populations of plants and animals have increased and decreased as a result of both natural events and human actions.

One example of a population that has changed over the years is fish. The waters off the shores of North America have supplied large quantities and varieties of fish. Overfishing and other abuses of the fishing areas have caused the populations to greatly decrease. But people are also taking action to protect the fish. In this investigation, you will model a population of codfish off the Grand Banks—a famous fishing area off the coast of Newfoundland, Canada. You will determine the effect of different events on that fish population.

1. Is a fishery a renewable resource or a nonrenewable resource? Explain your answer.

   _____

   _____

   _____

2. Aquaculture is the farming of water organisms. How might increased aquaculture of fish in an area help the local fisheries? How might it harm them?

   _____

   _____

   _____

Problem

How does a fish population change over time?

Safety 🛡️ *Review the safety guidelines in Appendix A of your textbook*
Use caution when cutting with scissors.

Living Resources • *Laboratory Investigation*

Procedure

1. As a group, make 8 "fish cards" from each sheet of colored paper, for a total of 64 cards. Write "Fish" on one side of each card. These fish cards represent the population of cod in fisheries off the Grand Banks. Each card represents many fish.

2. Divide a sheet of notebook paper in half. Label one half "Live Fish" and the other half "Dead Fish."

3. Obtain a set of event cards from your teacher. These cards represent events that can affect a fish population.

4. Shuffle and spread out the event cards, facedown. Count off 25 fish cards and place them by the notebook paper, as shown in Figure 1. Set the remaining 39 fish cards aside.

Figure 1

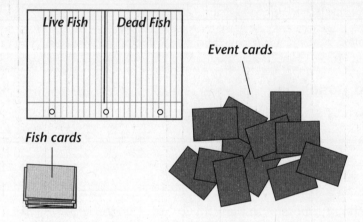

5. Pick up an event card. As a group, discuss and decide if the event you have chosen will likely increase or decrease the fish population.

6. If the event will increase the population, place a fish card from the stack of 25 on the Live Fish area of the notebook paper. If it will decrease the population, place a fish card on the Dead Fish area of the paper.

7. Replace the event card and mix up the event cards again.

8. Repeat this procedure until all 25 of the fish cards have been placed on either live or dead fish piles on the paper.

9. Count the number of live fish cards on the paper. Add half that number of fish cards from the remaining 39 cards to the live fish stack to represent additional fish added by reproduction. Remove the dead fish cards and set them aside with the remaining fish cards. Complete the Data Table in the Observations section for Generation 1.

10. The stack of live fish cards now represents the beginning of the second generation of fish. Repeat steps 5–9 to find out what happens to the second generation of fish.

11. Repeat steps 5–9 to find out what happens to the third generation of fish.

Living Resources · *Laboratory Investigation*

Managing Fisheries (continued)

Observations

Data Table

Starting number of fish cards: 25		
Generation	*Number of Live Fish Cards at End of Generation Before Reproduction*	*Number of Fish Cards After Reproduction*
1		
2		
3		

Analyze and Conclude

1. How did your fish population change over time?

   _____

   _____

   _____

2. Compare the numbers of fish at the end of each generation. Explain your results.

   _____

   _____

   _____

3. What are some ways this investigation models natural selection?

   _____

   _____

   _____

4. What are some ways in which natural selection differs from this model?

   _____

   _____

   _____

Living Resources ▪ *Laboratory Investigation*

Critical Thinking and Applications

1. How would fishing crews using a net with a large mesh affect the fish population compared to fishing crews using a net with a small mesh?

   _____

   _____

   _____

   _____

2. List two factors not listed in the questions or on the event cards that would affect the fish population.

   _____

   _____

3. Think about the effect that an increase in the predator population has on the fish population. Does this effect apply to all animal populations? Explain your answer.

   _____

   _____

   _____

More to Explore

Choose a different species to investigate. Make your own set of event cards and a data table. Be sure some events will likely increase the population and some will likely decrease it. Repeat the activity, using your event cards and data table. Write a paragraph explaining your results.